THE MODERN ORGAN GUIDE

A Resource for Buying an Organ or Keyboard Instrument in the 21ˢᵗ Century

Dr. Anthony,

Thanks for your invaluable assistance as I completed the project, especially the details of C.B. Fisk Opus 93. Continued blessings for your music ministry!

Chris

XULON PRESS

Psalm 150

Praise ye the Lord.
Praise God in his sanctuary:
praise him in the firmament of his power.
Praise him for his mighty acts;
praise him according to his excellent greatness.
Praise him with the sound of the trumpet:
praise him with the psaltery and harp.
Praise him with the timbrel and dance:
praise him with stringed instruments and organs.
Praise him upon the loud cymbals:
praise him upon the high-sounding cymbals.
Let everything that hath breath praise the Lord.
Praise ye the Lord.

In loving memory of my mother,

Mrs. Delores Coleman Riley
May 29, 1932 - October 15, 2005
(Oberlin College, Class of 1955)

Dedicated to the Riley Family:

Through many dangers, toils and snares
We have already come
'Twas grace that brought us safe thus-far
and grace will lead us on.

John Newton

Table of Contents

Prelude

My love for organ music and fascination with different types of organs has inspired me to write this book. I wanted to explore my interest in the organ, as well as provide a comprehensive resource for churches seeking new keyboard instruments. Growing up in a musical family, I was exposed to music at an early age. I was also raised in Union Memorial United Methodist Church in St. Louis, MO where my mother was a pianist and organist. Union Memorial is one of the oldest African American United Methodist churches west of the Mississippi river. The church then had an old Baldwin electronic organ built in the 1950's. With one keyboardist in the family, I was encouraged to select another instrument. I began violin lessons using the Suzuki method at the age of 10. I took violin lessons throughout middle school and continued to play in the high school orchestra as well as singing in the concert choir.

While in college, I continued to pursue my musical interests while majoring in ocean engineering at the United States Naval Academy (USNA). For four years, I sang in the USNA Protestant Chapel Choir and Gospel Choir. In these choirs, we sang great classical works as well as traditional and contemporary gospel repertoire. My interest in the pipe organ was further sparked by the great Moller pipe organ that majestically led the services at the Naval Academy Chapel. The Moller was a far cry from the Baldwin at my home church. While the chapel was being renovated in 1991, the pipe organ was also refurbished. During this time, a Rodgers digital organ took the place of the Moller for chapel services. The temporary Rodgers digital organ became my first exposure to state of the art electronic instruments. I was astounded by the quality of the pipe organ sound produced by the digital instrument.

I was also introduced to many other aspects of cutting edge technology in a broader sense than digital instruments. The engineering program included studies in physics, acoustics, electrical engineering, electronics and mechanical engineering. This background assisted me in understanding the technical aspect of sound generation and modern machinery. This knowledge has been very helpful in understanding modern keyboard instruments.

Acquiring a masters degree in mechanical engineering at Syracuse University further increased my knowledge in the engineering field. The two years there also allowed me to take pipe organ lessons from the chapel organist. My lessons there were held on the two three manual Holtkamp organs on the SU campus; one at Crouse College and the other at Hendricks Chapel. I later studied with the organist at a local community church which had a four manual Allen digital computer organ, which was one of Allen's most prestigious installations at that time. Later, while in the midst of submarine training, I continued organ studies on a three manual Austin pipe organ with the professor of organ at Connecticut College. After a four year hiatus due to serving on a Navy submarine, I resumed my study of organ in Virginia by playing various Rodgers, Hammond, Allen and Baldwin electronic organs. After moving to Groton, CT, I also had an opportunity to play an Austin pipe organ at Shepherd of the Seas chapel.

After collecting information on these and other organs for several years, I finally decided to write this book in 2001. Many books on the organ do not address the diversity of worship styles or the different instruments used in Christian churches today. On the other hand, many books celebrating the uniqueness of the African American worship experience focus on the music, but do not discuss the instruments used to make the music. The engineer in me wanted to explore some of the technology that was transforming the world of the organ in many ways. I also wanted to present a guide to churches who were in search of a new keyboard instrument. Having helped my home church purchase a new digital organ in 1992, I was familiar with the process and lack of objective resources. This book presents technical information about organs and keyboards in laymen's terms, and will expose you to a wide spectrum of keyboard instruments that are used in Christian worship settings today.

Chris Riley
Waldorf, MD
August, 2005

Acknowledgments

$\mathcal{I}$ could not have written this book without the help of many people across the country. I would have to begin with my parents who instilled in me the importance of excellence in all that I do. My mother, Mrs. Delores C. Riley, who dedicated herself to a career in music education, is the reason for my love for music. My father, Mr. Robert T. Riley, Sr. taught me that with a little bit of "gumption," I could achieve anything. Without them, I would never have been encouraged to appreciate a wide variety of musical genres. Both of my parents were gracious enough to read my manuscript in early forms and to provide meaningful feedback.

My wife Treska has had to live with me for the past five or so years of this musical odyssey. She has had to endure my endless musings about the book and to listen to my ever changing strategies for moving forward with its development. She not only has been faithful on accompanying me on numerous organ exploration expeditions (with our two small children), but has provided excellent feedback on the manuscript in its various stages.

I would like to thank many musicians who have contributed to my understanding of the organ. Most notably, those with whom I have studied include Dr. Katie Pardee, Mr. Scott Clark, Dr. John Anthony, and Dr. Ernest Brown. A special thanks is due to John Acker, Ken Brown and Ken Kohler, who have provided critical feedback on the technical accuracy of information pertaining to digital organs and encouraged me to continue writing. Rev. Nolan Williams, Jr. was instrumental in providing critical feedback and encouragement even in the midst of a challenging pipe organ selection process. As I neared the completion of the project, many people were especially helpful. Our pastor, Dr. Geoffrey V. Guns, encouraged me to come to an eventual point of closure in the writing process. Dr. John Barry Talley and Mr. Monte Maxwell were generous in providing information on the pipe organ at the Cathedral of the Navy. Dr. Mickey Thomas Terry provided insight during the final stages of writing. Additionally, special thanks to persons from the Allen Organ Company, Austin Organ Company, C.B. Fisk, Inc., Jordan Kitts and R. A. Daffer Organs, who gave us tours of their facilities.

Many other people have contributed in a variety of ways to the completion of this book. Some of their names appear in the pages that follow or on my website. I would like to think that in some way, this writing ties together people of different faiths, cultures, perspectives, and appreciation in the common interest in music that is a vital element of our worship of God.

Introduction

*A*t the writing of this book, we are in the beginning years of the 21st century. A review of the 20th century, reveals it as the century of great technological advances. The automobile was developed in the early part of the century, allowing a more reliable mechanical form of transportation. The development of the airplane has made cross-continental travel routine. The ability to tap into the unharnessed power of the atom has released the ability to power cities and propel vessels tirelessly through the ocean. By the end of the 20th century, these and other technological developments that were birthed in the beginning phases came to maturity.

The development of these technological advancements also impacted other aspects of society. Crude radios and phonographs that transported music, the spoken word and narrative of sporting events over miles developed into digital recordings and compact disks that provided unprecedented fidelity of sound. The advancements in sound recording and reproduction occurred along with the corresponding increased understanding of electronics. Not only was music and its reproduction transformed, but the instruments used to create the music were impacted by the new technology.

This book was written to explore the development of the organ, which has been called the "King of Instruments." The organ went through a drastic transformation in the 20th century because of the technologies discussed previously, especially in the field of electronics. As the technology of sound improved, these electronic developments were infused in the organ. Pipe organs of the early 20th century were being challenged by digital electronic organs by century's end. The first electronic organs were developed in the early 20th century, about the time the radio itself was entering adolescence. Similarly, the acoustic piano was eventually challenged by digital keyboard instruments.

Although the pipe organ dominated the musical scene in the early 20th century, it has been replaced in many cases by digital electronic organs or keyboards. A corresponding shift in the educational focus of schools of music has not been made. Most leading universities and conservatories today still focus instruction on the pipe organ or piano, and indoctrinate students of such instruments in the repertoire of tradition. The world of academia has not responded in total to the shift in technological focus of these keyboard instruments.

Unlike academia, the Christian church, the primary purveyor of organ music and the instrument itself, has followed the trend of technology more so than tradition. The church as a whole has undergone a tremendous transformation through the 20th century. The Catholic Church has been modernized by Vatican II, and mainline Protestant denominations (Lutherans, Methodists, Episcopalians and Presbyterians) are on the decline. These churches have been overcome by a wave of new nondenominational gatherings that have chosen to abandon not only the traditional church's dogma, but its music as well. The music of the church, which was once markedly sacred in character, has now taken on the rhythms and cadences of secular culture.

The music of the church today has become as diverse as the people that make up its ranks. Gospel music has interjected itself into the church. Songs which speak more of a relationship with God than theological tenets, and which carry distinctive ethnic influences of the cultures that produced them, have become increasingly popular in the church today. The formal classical anthems of yesterday have been joined by praise and worship music, which exuberantly celebrates the faith with great fervor.

These new musical forms have been accompanied by variations on the theme of the traditional pipe organ and piano. The Hammond organ and other electronic organs were developed in the early 1900's. Electronic keyboards came to prominence in the 1970's, and were standardized by the development of the Musical Instrument Digital Interface (MIDI) in the 1980's. Because of the technological developments that transformed civilization, elements of the above mentioned keyboard instruments have been intertwined at the advent of the 21st century. Pipe organs and digital electronic organs have been joined together to produce combined sound. These organs are capable of playing Hammond organ sounds, or the palette of sounds available from standard MIDI voices. Much will be said about these instruments later in the book. These new instruments can be found used in popular music of secular culture as well as increasingly in the music of the church.

Much of the current church growth literature expresses a link between church growth and the incorporation of contemporary music. This theory is based on the assertion that people can be best evangelized by the familiar music which pervades secular culture.[1] Equally important is worship that is exuberant in contrast to the relatively reserved and sedate worship of the traditional service. At some point in the growth of a church, the electronic keyboard instruments used in contemporary worship may not be able to compete with the tens of thousands of people that fill worship centers of today's mega-churches. In contrast to largely amplified electronic instruments, the pipe organ is actually the only instrument that can assert itself above the voices of thousands of people singing at once. This may be the case with the Yoido Full Gospel Church is Seoul, South Korea, which installed a very large pipe organ in 2000. Yoido Church is the largest church in the world with an estimated membership of over 750,000 people. Sunday worship services have attendance of over 40,000.[2] The reality is that the pipe organ can play many types of music and is the only instrument that is powerful enough to lead thousands of people in song.

Churches like Yoido Full Gospel have changed the face of Christianity. The climate of worship in the Christian church today is like never before. This is true throughout the world in addition to America. Not only do we see a tremendous diversity, but the advances of technology present more musical instrument options. Many churches today find themselves looking to purchase a new organ or other keyboard instrument for a variety of reasons. First, older pipe organs may be in need of maintenance and repair. Older electronic organs have been superseded by better quality instruments and are being replaced. Some of these older instruments are no longer musically reliable. Many churches today are moving into new buildings due to rapid growth. These congregations may not be able to bring their existing instrument into the new edifice. Each day, new churches are being founded across the country. These new congregations are also in need of purchasing instruments as aids to worship. Finally, traditional churches have made some degree of transition to at least include more gospel or contemporary music. In order to do so, new instruments may be desired.

Unfortunately, there are very few resources available that can objectively assist churches in purchasing a new instrument, and appreciate the great diversity that exists within these churches as a whole. Most traditional churches have at least one trained organist as part of their music ministry. These musicians may have ample training and exposure to the pipe organ and are able to select a new instrument if required. However, the vast majority of musicians and the instruments they play are not confined to the strictest definition of liturgical music. These musicians may consider pipe organs, electronic organs, drawbar organs and MIDI keyboards as equally viable aids to worship.

This book is designed primarily to be a resource for church organ committees who are engaged in the process of searching for a new instrument. Every attempt is made to respect the denominational and ethnic diversity within the Christian church in America that requires a wide variety of keyboard instruments. To assist members of the committee who may not be musicians, a brief history of the organ will be presented. This includes the history of the pipe organ in America as well as their electronic counterparts. After this background information, the process to be used by the organ committee is explored. The major pipe and digital organ companies in the U.S. are also presented. This is followed by a review of the broad spectrum of instruments that may be found in churches of denominations across the country. Additional reference information is contained in the appendix that is designed to assist the organ committee or individual musicians.

My hope is that this book will provide insight into an aspect of Christian worship that is very diverse. Certainly, at the beginning of the 21st century we are at an awesome time in history. We are at a point in which tradition has been challenged by the contemporary culture. This tension is clearly apparent within the different modes of worship used in Christian churches. Additionally, we see an equally vast contrast between traditional instruments such as the pipe organ, contemporary keyboards and MIDI. Many worship settings today include music that reaches across generational lines. Recognizing this diversity, this book considers the vast scope of keyboard instruments that could be used in worship today. Sufficient information is presented to give members of a selection process a good understanding of the options that are available to them today. The instruments used are vital components of the music ministry of any church.

This book was written to provide information where academia has left off regarding keyboard instruments. More music departments at colleges and universities are offering courses on transformational technologies in music, such as MIDI and digital sound generation. As stated before, most formal music training focuses on the traditional music and its instruments. This book is intended to review the traditional pipe organ, and understand the technological developments that have transformed it over the past 100 years. Additionally, other electronic organs and keyboard instruments that have been developed during the 20th century will be discussed.

CHAPTER 1:

The Music Ministry and
the Instrument Selection Process

$\mathcal{T}$he overall church mission or vision is a key starting point in understanding the role of the music ministry. The vision of the music ministry must be in harmony with the vision of the overall ministry. This vision should be clearly articulated through the leadership of pastor and director of music. The long term vision of the music ministry will be a determining factor in the musicians as well as instruments that are utilized in the ministry. The needs of the music ministry incorporate several factors that are impacting churches today. These include changing ministry styles, contemporary musicians and transitioning to new worship centers or sanctuaries. Any of these changes can create a demand within the music ministry for new instruments.

A church may find itself in one of several situations regarding its instruments. Due to the above mentioned changes in the music ministry, the church may be looking to add a different type of organ or keyboard instrument. Older instruments may need to be replaced or upgraded if moving to a new edifice. The purchase of a MIDI keyboard or Hammond organ may be desired if a shift to a more contemporary form of worship is desired.

A church may decide to form a committee that will spearhead the selection of new instruments. It is unlikely that any given church would have within its membership five to ten trained organists. Yet, when most churches embark upon the journey of selecting a new organ for their sanctuary, they may form a committee of knowledgeable persons. The size of the committee can vary depending on the policies of the church and the scope of the project. On the small side, the committee could be comprised of the pastor, director of music, and a trustee or deacon. For a more complex project, the committee could also include several musicians, organist, choir members, an organ consultant, trustees, and architectural consultants. Regardless of the size of the committee, it is useful for the group to understand the process that they will be involved in when searching for any type of keyboard instrument.

The organ committee has an awesome responsibility. The result of this committee's work may produce an organ once in a 50 year period. In some cases, an organ may last over a century. When entering this organ selection process, the committee should use a structured process in order to make a wise choice that fits the church's immediate and future needs. The selection committee must start with the vision of the church and music ministry in specific as a framework for their task. If the committee desires an instrument that can lead congregational hymns and accompany the choir for singing anthems, they might consider a different instrument than what would be appropriate if praise and worship music is used in the services. If the ministry is looking to incorporate more praise and worship music, they may not be in the market for a new pipe organ. The committee also must decide what the space limitations are where the organ will be installed. Some sanctuaries or auditoriums may preclude the use of real pipes, or at least for some pedal voices. Certainly, the budget for the project is another determining factor. If a donor has bequeathed several million dollars for the purchase of a fine pipe organ, the process will be quite different from that of a congregation working with limited funds. Finally, the schedule for acquiring the instrument is very important. If a new instrument is needed within several months, the committee has an urgent task at hand. However, if a large building project is being planned concurrent with the need for the instrument, several years may be allowed to plan and procure the instrument.

The following steps can be used by any organ committee, regardless of church size and funds available.

Instrument Selection Committee Procedure

1. Decide that an organ or keyboard is needed or desired.
2. Determine if an organ committee will be formulated and if an organ consultant is desired/required.
3. Familiarize committee members with organ or keyboard basics if non-musicians are participants in the selection process. (Chapters 2 through 5)
4. Determine the musical need for organ using Appendix A Organ Committee Guide
   a. main purpose
   b. additional purposes
   c. skill level of organists who will play the organ (now and in future)
   d. select an instrument that will attract or keep a qualified organist
5. Establish a budget.
6. Determine schedule requirements for the instrument. How urgent is the need?
7. Conduct Research on organs/keyboards (Chapters 2 through 5):
   a. review types of organs within interest window
   b. identify organ dealers/builders in immediate area
   c. identify other organs in immediate area that may be of interest to hear or play
   d. identify and contact other organists who can offer an unbiased opinion
8. Get detailed information about each company (Chapter 6):
   a. establish a point of contact
   b. conduct preliminary online research
   c. what is the company's main focus?
   d. does the company sell/build organs exclusively?
   e. what support services does the company offer?
   f. how many years of experience do they have?
   g. has the company installed other organs in the immediate area?
9. Meet the organ dealer representative at their facility and conduct a tour.
10. Listen to their instruments played. Ensure that the church

organist can play the instruments themselves. Pay attention to the overall sound quality rather than special features. (It is best to listen to an organ installed in a sanctuary or auditorium over the organ company showroom.)

11. Work with each company's representative to determine what they would recommend for your church's needs.
12. Obtain proposals from a variety of builders/dealers.
13. Decide which company will be selected to provide the instrument.
14. Sign contract to purchase organ/keyboard and begin construction (if required).
15. Instrument is installed and voiced by the company. (Some companies assemble pipe organs at their factory prior to shipping.)
16. Schedule and conduct the organ dedication concert.
17. Identify and schedule regular maintenance and tuning for the instrument.

The instrument selection process is a challenging task for any church to undertake. The complexity of the project is largely dependent on the size of the instrument desired. Many other factors are involved which can add to the complexity. These factors include the skill level of musicians, musical desires for the organ, budget, available finances, urgency of need, use of an existing organ and physical location of the new instrument (existing sanctuary, new edifice, etc.). Most importantly, it should be understood that the task of selecting and installing an instrument is a *process*, one which has distinct steps.

Step 1-The first step in the process is the decision that a new instrument is needed or that an existing instrument needs to be upgraded. This need may be due to a variety of factors. A church may be building a new edifice and in need of a larger instrument. The church may be using an older instrument that no longer fits their needs, or is no longer reliable. New musical tastes may require a more versatile instrument. In some cases, a large financial donation may have been given to the church in order to purchase a new organ. In any case, the first step is the realization that a new or upgraded organ is needed.

Step 2-The leadership of the church (to include pastor, director or minister of music and trustees) may next decide that a committee may be needed to spearhead the organ selection process. For most churches, this process is too difficult for one person to conduct themselves. The above mentioned leadership core may also include additional members to comprise the committee. These additional persons may include organist or pianist, choir members, deacons, other trustees, or a professional organ consultant. The organ consultant may be a professional organist who is a member of the American Guild of Organists (AGO) or someone who is recognized as an expert in the field of the organ. Eventually, the representatives of the organ firm that has been selected to install the instrument will serve as organ consultants.

Step 3-The next phase in the process should be for members of the committee to be introduced to the organ in general. Some members of the committee may be selected for their fiscal expertise and not be familiar with the organ. Pastors themselves are not introduced to the specifics of the organ in their theological training. Some musicians also may not be familiar with the most current information available concerning church organs. This variation in level of knowledge concerning the organ necessitates some type of familiarity training to establish a baseline understanding of the organ for members of the committee. This book was written to do just that: to establish a baseline level of knowledge for members of organ committees who are involved in the organ selection process. Many other resources are available which can supplement this book and are mentioned in the Bibliography.

Unfortunately, many churches omit this step and begin contacting organ company representatives before formulating a coherent team. This premature contact may result in the church getting locked in one particular path (one specific organ company or type of organ) due to not taking the time to investigate all of their options and identify their real needs. With the aid of this book, much of the committee's work can be accomplished without even contacting specific organ companies. Having better information will allow the committee to make a better decision about what company and which instrument is able to meet all of their needs.

Step 4-Probably the most important factor is the musical need. The committee can begin the selection process by considering the musical need for the instrument. The committee must consider the music ministry of the church and determine its focus. The church may be more traditional and feature classical music and frequent organ concerts. The church may be more culturally diverse and include gospel or contemporary music in additional to the classical repertoire. If the church is exclusively gospel or contemporary in musical tastes, it will be in the market for yet a different type of organ or keyboard. The skill level of the musician is another strong factor which may be closely related to the type of music featured by the music program. For example, a musician who has a degree in organ performance may not be very satisfied with a MIDI keyboard. Conversely, a musician who only plays by ear probably does not need a large custom pipe organ to express the range of their repertoire.

Step 5-The committee must understand the fiscal limitations of their charter. This clearly defines the budget unless other funds are available. If the funds are not available, the church may have a target cost that is part of a fundraising plan. This scenario will rely more heavily on the schedule of when the organ is needed. The budget ranges can be separated into several levels from small to very large. The following summarizes the various budget ranges:

Small: less than $50,000

Medium: $50,000-$100,000

Large: $100,000-$500,000

Very Large: greater than $500,000

Being within one of these ranges narrows the focus of instruments that are available. Within the small budget range, small to medium digital organs are available. The medium budget range opens the options up to used pipe organs and large digital organs. The large budget range makes available very large custom digital organs and moderately sized pipe organs. The very large range extends the range into the purchase of large pipe organs. Very large new pipe organs may cost as much as several million dollars. The committee must also consider funds available for periodic maintenance and tuning of pipe organs.

Step 6-The next factor to be considered is the schedule or time frame in which the new organ is needed. This factor parallels budget and is usually directly related to the budget. An instrument that costs more (especially in the very large budget category) may take several years of fundraising to finance. Most pipe organ companies have a wait of at least 3 to 5 years to design and build a new organ. This lead time often provides sufficient time for a church to complete fundraising for the organ. A church that is building a new edifice may also have several years of planning, design and construction to be completed before the new organ is needed. The committee should keep the long-term needs of the church or organization in mind when considering cost and schedule:

- Will they want to purchase a pipe organ that could be in service for at least 50 years or more if maintained properly?
- Will they be content with a digital instrument that may require replacement in 20 to 30 years?
- Are they willing to make the investment in a long-term instrument or are other financial interests more pressing for their ministry or organization?
- Would a combination instrument meet their immediate needs and allow for addition of more pipe ranks over time?
- Will they want to purchase an instrument that will be used by generations to come, succumb to the latest musical fad, or satisfy a short-term need?

Schedule requirements for the organ project can also be categorized, similar to the budget. An urgent need for an organ is one that is required within six months. In this case, a moderate digital instrument would be appropriate. If the need date is between six months and one year, a customized digital instrument possibly combined with pipes would be possible. This would reflect a moderate schedule need. If the organ is not needed for 3 to 5 years, this category is long-term. Enough time is available to select a custom pipe instrument in this case. Additionally, a church with a long-term need may consider the temporary use of a digital organ while their custom pipe organ is being built.

Step 7-The internet can be a source of a great deal of information for the organ committee. Without making a phone call or leaving the church, a tremendous amount of information can be attained about any type of organ and the companies that manufacture and sell them. Most organ builders and individual dealers have websites. A comprehensive list is found in Appendix D. These sites often contain contact information as well as pertinent facts about the company to include company history, philosophy, a description of their instruments, and vision for the future. The sites usually present information on their instruments, to include pictures and stop lists. Most company sites also contain information about noted installations, which normally contains pictures and stop lists of the installed feature instruments.

The internet is also a good source for reference material about the organ and other keyboard instruments. Many important professional organizations related to the organ have excellent websites that can be good sources of information. These organizations include the American Guild of Organists, individual AGO chapters, and the Organ Historical Society. The organ committee should spend as much time as possible gathering information from the internet before contacting individual companies. This may allow the committee members to become familiar with the task at hand in addition to some of their options before being bombarded with material from company representatives. Quite possibly, the committee may be able to formulate a plan before embarking upon this great task.

Step 8-Once the musical need, skill level of musician(s), budget, and schedule have been determined, the committee should have formulated several options. This understanding will help them determine which organ companies may be able to meet their needs. The descriptions of organ companies found later in this book will be very helpful in determining the major focus, strengths and weaknesses of organ companies that are in business today. This may be particularly important if the church is in a more remote area in which no organ companies are located. The committee would be wasting their time and that of the company representatives to pursue a company whose instruments would not fit their needs.

Step 11-The architectural specifics of the building (sanctuary or worship center) in which the organ will be located are important to consider. This is a point of widely varying opinion and confusion.

The organ consultant or representatives from the organ company should be able to adequately address these concerns. A large organ (more than three manuals or 50 stops) is not necessarily required in a large building that seats 1000 or more people. A pipe organ allows adjustment of voicing all stops to include the wind pressure that is used to fit a particular space. The acoustics of the space is also important to consider. A smaller instrument in a space with better acoustics may actually sound "larger" than a large instrument in an acoustically dead space. Factors which affect the acoustics of the room include size and shape, shape of ceiling, height of ceiling, carpeting, wall surfaces and location of the organ pipes or speakers. The committee should keep in mind that beyond three manuals and 50 stops, additional manuals and stops add more to the variety and flexibility of the instrument and not the loudness of the instrument. A three-manual instrument is more than satisfactory for most average musicians, music programs and buildings. Fourth and fifth manuals may add more variety of stops and additional solo voices or an Antiphonal or Positiv division, but are by no means necessary. For example, the three-manual Aeolian-Skinner organ at Trinity Church in Boston boasts over 100 stops in 11 divisions.

Step 12-Once the needs of the church have been articulated to the instrument company representative through the committee, the company presents a proposal. Depending on the complexity of the project, the solicitation may involve the participation of more than one company. For example, incorporating a new digital instrument may include pipe work by a pipe organ company and digital voices by a digital organ company.

Steps 13 and 14-The committee reviews the proposals from different companies and selects the one that meets their needs. By returning to the team's charter, team members may be able to rate the different proposals on how well the proposal satisfies the identified needs. In addition to installation and voicing, the team should consider support services such as maintenance and warranty. The contract should be awarded to the company that is best able to provide an instrument that meets the church's needs and is within the budget for the project. The team should also consider their perception of company representatives because the church is establishing a long-term relationship with the company. The committee should focus on the important factors such as sound, quality and ease of maintenance. While evaluating the different benefits of each organ, they must keep in mind the bottom line. Are they choosing an instrument that is musically satisfying, that meets their musical needs and is within their budget?

Steps 14 and 15-The committee enters the process of installing the new instrument after entering into contract with the selected company or companies. This may include removing an old instrument, fabrication of parts for the new instrument or moving an older instrument to a new location with upgrades. If a person with project management experience is a member of the team or of the church, they may be useful in tracking the progress of the project. An assessment should be given through the project of adherence to the planned budget and schedule. An experienced organist may be able to evaluate the quality of work during the project as well.

Step 16-The end of the execution phase could culminate with the dedication concert if desired. A selected musical artist should be scheduled well in advance to ensure the concert is conducted flawlessly.

Step 17-The committee's work has not completed once the dedication concert has been conducted. The team may need to meet periodically to assess any maintenance concerns as time progresses. Periodic maintenance and tuning is especially vital if pipes are part of the instrument. This maintenance may be part of the original contract or may need to be negotiated separately.

CHAPTER 2:

Organ Basics

*T*his section is designed to familiarize members of the organ committee with the organ. The information presented may be especially useful for pianists or vocalists who may not have been exposed to the pipe organ in the course of their training. This will be helpful for members of the committee who are not musicians. The most basic information is presented to explain the pipe organ in general and the layout of the standard pipe organ console. A general explanation of the different stops on an organ is presented in order to explain what these different 'voices' are. A brief description of the Hammond organ is also provided because of its differences from a pipe organ. A glossary is also included later in the book which defines many important terms related to organs today.

Organ History in Brief

The pipe organ evolved from pan pipes or flutes that date back thousands of years ago to the days of the ancient Egyptian and ancient Greece. The pipes were originally blown by the musician in order to make the desired sound. The modern organ has evolved from an instrument that used a hydraulic pump to provide pressure for the instrument. An instrument called the hydraulis may have been used in Alexandria in the 300 B.C. Along with other Egyptian developments, the Romans apparently developed the use of the hydraulis, and used the instrument in their entertainment and sporting events.[1]

The hydraulis was developed in Europe and became known as the organ. Over time, craftsmen have allowed the organ to make different sounds by using pipes constructed of different materials and using different shapes. An hydraulic pump has been replaced by a blower. The organ has remained essentially unchanged from the 18th century on. The pipe organ of the 17th and 18th century was mainly comprised of ranks of principals, mixtures and flute pipes. During the Baroque period, much of classical organ music was composed by Bach, Buxtehude and other greats. String sounds and solo reed stops were not used in organs until later in the 19th century. Interestingly, organs in England did not have a pedal board until the 19th century. Organs in the late 19th and early 20th century saw the inclusion of string stops and solo voices which were featured in the more Romantic music of that period.

Organ Crawl

The organ produces sound by forcing air pressurized by a blower through different pipes. The keyboards are used to control the pipes so that as a key is depressed, air is introduced into the corresponding pipe. The stops are the individual voices of the organ. Each stop has its own sound, and can be used in combinations to produce a desired effect. The term 'organ crawl' has been used to describe the process of literally crawling through the spaces of an organ chamber where the pipes are found. In this case, we will apply the term to exploring the organ console and the speaker chambers for electronic organs. An organ can be an imposing sight.

The Organ Console

Each keyboard, referred to as a manual, normally has 61 keys and controls a different part of the organ. Some organ manual keyboards may have as few as 56 keys. The sounds on each of the manuals can even be coupled together for added flexibility. The keys consist of white naturals and black sharps, usually made of wood or plastic material. Keyboards can be special ordered with walnut sharps, or a combination of maple naturals and rosewood sharps. Even more elaborate materials such as ivory or bone can be selected. American pedalboards are made of 32 notes (some have as few as 30), and usually are concaved and radiating. The Pedal plays the bass notes in a music score and provides the foundation for the organs' music. The stops selected on the manuals can also be coupled to the Pedal.

The Basics of Organ Registration

Registration is the art of selecting appropriate stops for different pieces of music. There are four main categories of stops on an organ: principal or diapason, flute, string and reed. Many of these stops can be found on multiple manual or pedal divisions of the organ. On the two-manual organ, the bottom manual is the Great, and the top is the Swell. On French organs and French-styled instruments, the Great (Grand-orgue) is the lowest manual. On the three-manual organ, the bottom manual is the Choir or Positiv, the middle manual is the Great, and the top manual is the Swell. The Positiv division is usually smaller than a Choir division, is not enclosed and contains no string stops. The four-manual organ has the same keyboard arrangement as the three-manual organ, but the top manual is the solo. A large five-manual organ may have an additional Positiv or Antiphonal division played by the fifth manual. The manuals can be played independently or coupled to each other or to the Pedal.

The pitch level of each stop in the organ is expressed in terms of the speaking length of the lowest pipe (low C) in the rank. A rank is the set of pipes that correspond to a particular stop (see Glossary). On an organ with 61-note keyboards, there are 61 pipes per rank. The pedal board has 32 notes and therefore a Pedal stop rank contains 32 pipes. A stop marked 8' controls a rank of pipes that sound at unison pitch, that is, pitches corresponding to those of a piano. The number 8 is used because an open pipe which sounds the lowest note of an 8' stop (low C) is about eight feet long. Pipes in a rank become progressively shorter as they ascend in pitch, and at every octave they halve in length. Pipes also become smaller in diameter as they get shorter. The pipe that sounds tenor C, an octave higher than 8' C, is one-half as long, or 4 feet. The pipe sounding middle C is two feet long, and the pipe lengths of the remaining C's of an 8' stop are one foot, one-half foot, and one-quarter foot. Therefore, a stop marked 4' sounds an octave higher than an 8' stop. A stop marked 2' sounds two octaves higher. A 16' stop sounds an octave lower and a 32' stop sounds two octaves lower than an 8' stop.

The basic stop on the organ is the principal or diapason. The sound produced by this stop is uniquely characteristic to the organ. No other instrument produces this sound. The main ensemble is called the principal chorus. This is made using principal stops at different pitch levels corresponding to the main octave. The principal chorus is made up of principal stops at the 8', 4' and 2' pitches. The mixture stops are compound stops of multiple ranks of high-pitched principal pipes that add brilliance, intensity and clarity to the principal chorus. MIXTURE stops include the Mixture, Scharf, Fourniture or Plein-Jeu.

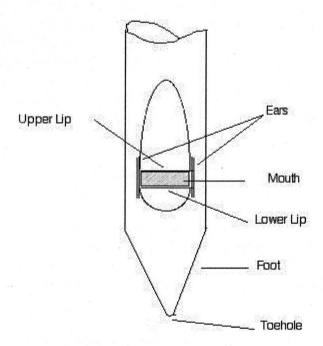

Figure 1. Diagram of Flue Pipe

Another family of stops are flute stops. These stops sound very much like orchestral flutes and have a smooth sound. They can be used to accompany solo stops, or to give the principal chorus a fuller sound. Examples of flute stops are the Bourdon, Gedackt, Rohrflöte, and Koppelflöte. The mutation stops are derivations of the principal or flute stops. They are used to add brilliance to the principal chorus, or in combination with flute stops to form colorful solo voices. Figure 1 illustrates the components of the flue pipe, which includes principals or diapasons, strings and flute pipes. An excellent description of the operation of flue and reed pipes is found in <u>The Organists' Manual</u> by Roger Davis. This book also contains additional diagrams of flue pipes, reed pipes and many pictures of each. In addition to the stops that sound unison and octave pitches, there are principal and flute mutation stops which produce pitches corresponding to the off-unison partials of the harmonic series.

The Hammond organ is built to produce tones that are similar to a flute. The tone wheels used to produce the sound are capable of producing pitches from 16' to 1' and include mutations 5 1/3', 2 2/3' and 1 1/3'. In this way, the Hammond organ follows the same harmonic structure as the pipe organ, but the tone generation is limited to the flute sound.

The next class of stops are reed stops. These stops are mainly found in the Swell and Pedal, although several may be found in the Great and Choir. These stops can be used as solo stops in a fanfare. Chorus reeds are used with full organ to add power to the ensemble. Stops in the Swell include the Trompette, Fagott and Waldhorn. Stops in the Pedal include Contra Bombarde, Contra Posaune, Fagott, Tuba and Clarion.

The Swell organ also contains most of the String stops. These stops have a sound similar to the string instruments of the orchestra. Examples of these types of stops are the Viole, Viole da Gamba, and Viola Celeste. They are used to accompany solo voices or as soft background music. Occasionally, they can be used with the principal stops to add warmth and create a variety of sound. The celeste voices (string or flute) are usually tuned slightly sharp, so as to produce a beating effect when played with the parent stop.

The last category of stops are the solo stops, which are mainly found in the solo division on large organs. They include the French Horn, English Horn, Trompette, Tuba, Tuba Miribalis and Trompette en Chamade. Registration for hymn playing would include the principal chorus. The Mixture stop could be added for brilliance, and one of the solo stops could be used to play the melody or a descant for a particular verse. There are many schools of thought when registration is concerned. In any case, there is some room for artistic interpretation, especially if a more gospel sound is desired. This may include the use of the Tremulant on the manuals with the principal, String and or flute stops drawn. In classical registration, the Tremulant is only to be used with solo stops such as the Oboe or the Cornet flute stop combination. A Registration Guide can be found in Appendix B to provide additional information on stops and to summarize organ stop names from various countries.[2]

The Organ

The pipe organ is comprised of all of the pipes that make up the instrument. The pipes are grouped in different divisions called Great, Swell, Positiv or Choir and Pedal. The organ voices within each of these groups were discussed in the previous section on registration. The pipes in the Great organ make up the core of the organ. These pipes are usually principal or diapason pipes, which are unique to the organ. The Great organ pipes are normally exposed and not found in an enclosure. The Swell pipes are contained in an enclosure called the 'Swell box'. The opening in the Swell box is filled with Swell shades, which can be opened or closed to control the volume of the sound coming from the Swell pipes. The Great and Swell are played from separate keyboards or manuals. The bass pipes for the organ are contained in the Pedal division. The Pedal division is similar to the Great in that it is not enclosed and contains similar pipe voices. These pipes can play up several octaves lower than the manuals. The Pedal keyboard or clavier is located under the manual keyboards and is played with the feet while the organist sits on the organ bench. Most standard organs contain the Great, Swell and Pedal divisions as a minimum. Larger organs could contain a third manual division called either the Choir or the Positiv. The pipes in this division comprise voices that are softer than those of the Great and may be an octave higher in pitch. The Choir division is normally enclosed similar to the Swell, while the Positiv division is not enclosed. Very large organs may contain a fourth or fifth manual division called the solo or antiphonal division. Solo divisions contain pipe ranks that simulate orchestral sounds that can be used as solo voices.

Organ Stop Controls

The organ console is the 'nerve center' for the organ. The organists sits at the organ bench of the console and is able to operate all of the controls for the organ. One of the most noticeable features of the organ console is that it has more than one keyboard as well as foot Pedals. Organ stop controls are found in several configurations. Most traditionally, stop jambs are found on each side of the manuals. The stop jambs contain the drawknobs that operate each stop. The drawknobs for the Pedal and Swell organ are found to the left of the keyboards. The drawknobs for the Great and Choir/Positiv organ are located to the right of the keyboards. The names of each stop voice are engraved on the front face of the drawknob. There are several modes of operation of the drawknobs: one is mechanical and the other is lighted. On some organs, the stops are selected by pulling out the corresponding drawknob, thus the term "pulling out all the stops." On certain organs with a lighted capture system, the drawknob face lights when pulled out, and springs back into position. To deselect a stop in both cases, the drawknob is simply pushed in. In some organs, the stops are arranged above the manuals in a tilt tab or rocker tab arrangement. When the tab corresponding to the desired stop is switched down, the stop is selected. Lighted capture systems have rocker tabs, which light when the stop is selected.

The Hammond Organ uses drawbars to control each voice. In reality, it is the first organ to allow the organist to control each stop individually in real time. Each drawbar can be adjusted to a level from 0 to 10. This control allows the intensity of each fundamental tone to be controlled. For example, adjusting the 8' drawbar on a Hammond is like voicing an 8' flute stop on a pipe organ. Hammond organ presets are located to the left of the manuals. They are arranged as a reverse-colored keyboard of one octave. Each key is a different preset that allows drawbar combinations to be accessed. Based on the harmonic structure of the actual instrument, the Hammond drawbars can also be adjusted to simulate orchestral sounds and even a principal stop. This flexibility is one of the strongest features of the Hammond organ.

Figure 2. Four-Manual M.P. Moller Console
(U.S. Naval Academy Chapel, Annapolis, MD)

On the vertical section below each manual are numbered buttons. These control presets for the organ. This allows the organist to save combinations of stops for a variety of organ registrations. General presets control stops for the entire organ, while divisional control stops for each manual or the Pedal. For example, there may be 5 divisional pistons for the Swell, which only control combinations of stops for the Swell division. Again, some organs have lighted controls. Stops selected to be played on the organ manuals can be coupled together or to the Pedal. These controls are normally found on rocker tabs above the manuals. They are also found on pistons next to the divisional presets. Numerous other controls can be found as pistons. These include Tutti or Sforzando, Memory level, Melody Coupler, Bass Coupler and Flute Vibrato. The Tutti or Sforzando control brings on full organ immediately. The Melody Coupler allows a solo stop from the Swell to be played automatically on the top note played on the Great manual. Similarly, the Bass Coupler allows the lowest note on the Great to be played on the Pedal. These features allow a pianist to play the organ like a piano, and sound like an organ virtuoso.

Many of these controls are paralleled in toe studs found on the vertical section of the organ above the Pedals. Here one finds toe studs for the general controls, divisional controls, and usually reversibles for 32' Pedal stops. The expression pedals for the organ are found in the center of this panel. Although most pipe organs do not have an expression Pedal for the Great, this is common for electronic organs. The Swell organ expression Pedal is normally in the middle, and the far right Pedal is the crescendo expression Pedal, which causes more stops to be drawn leading up to full organ.

Digital/Electronic and Combination Organs

Electronic organs are different from pipe organs because their sound is produced from sound generators and emanates from speakers instead of pipes. The pipes are both the sound generators and amplifiers. Older electronic organs used vacuum tubes or transistors to produce the various sounds of the organ which simulated the same sounds from pipe organs. Since the digital revolution, voices from real pipe organs have been recorded and are the source of the organ's sound. The console of electronic organs is virtually identical to that of pipe organs. Hammond organs are electronic organs as well but are different from pipe organs or their electronic counterparts. The Hammond organ will be discussed in detail later.

Combination organs have sounds that are produced by pipes as well as electronic means. This has been a recent development, becoming predominant since the 1990's. The organ console can be used to play both the pipe and electronic voices together. In newer combination instruments, the pipe and electronic voices are nearly indistinguishable. In these organs, the foundation stops (diapasons, principals, flutes) are from real pipes, while some of the unique voices (Strings, solo stops) are from electronic sources. The combination instrument provides a means of having a larger organ at a minimized cost because electronic voices are more affordable than real pipes. The challenge for the combination organ is to ensure the pipe voices stay in tune with the electronic ones.

The Traditional Organist

The traditional church organist may be somewhat of an endangered species. Compared to 50 years ago, the pipe organ is not the mainstay of many church music programs. In many cases, the person playing the organ may actually be a pianist, and have little or no formal pipe organ training. The church may not even have an organ; they may use a very contemporary praise band. In any case, anyone who plays the organ should have basic understanding of organ registration. The skill level of the organist may vary from someone without formal training to a person with years of formal training who is the president of the local chapter of the American Guild of Organists. Whatever the skill level, each person should be committed to continual improvement, always seeking to develop themselves and improve their playing.

The most famous organist throughout history is certainly J.S. Bach, who lived and composed music during the Baroque period of the 1700's. Most people would immediately recognize his famous Toccata in D minor. The leading composer of organ music during the Baroque period, his organ works are the core of standard repertoire of serious organ students. Of contemporary American organists, Virgil Fox probably had the greatest influence on the spread of organ music. Serving as the organist at Riverside Church in New York City for many years, Fox's 'Heavy Organ' concerts at Carnegie

Hall in the 1970's had a profound influence on the widespread appreciation of the organ. With the help of the Rodgers and Allen Organ Companies, he continued his career as a concert organist on tour. His final mark on the organ world is the mammoth Hazel Wright Organ at the Crystal Cathedral, which incorporated an Aeolian-Skinner Organ from Lincoln Center. Designed by Fox, the organ was built by Fratelli Ruffatti in 1987.[3]

On the other end of the spectrum was E. Power Biggs. Biggs was a champion of the Neo-baroque movement in the 1940's and favored a departure from the romantic organs of the early 20th century. He was a staunch purist and was initially supportive of the American Classic movement led by G. Donald Harrison of Aeolian-Skinner Organ Company. Biggs was instrumental in working with Harrison on the Boston Symphony Hall Organ in 1947 and in the revoicing of the Methuen Memorial Hall Organ in 1953. In the mid 1950's, a rift developed between Biggs and Harrison. In 1954, Biggs traveled to Europe to investigate important pipe organs in the continent. As a result, he shifted from supporting the American Classic movement to the Neo-baroque movement. He found organs with tracker controls much more applicable to the music of J.S. Bach than their electro-pneumatic counterparts. His alliances with organ builders also shifted to Flentrop from Holland and Charles B. Fisk of Massachusetts. Biggs was also a firm opponent of the electronic organ and vehemently opposed the installation of a Rodgers electronic organ in Carnegie Hall (designed in part by Virgil Fox) instead of the Flentrop pipe organ.[4]

No organist today seems to dominate the landscape of American organ music in the way that Biggs and Fox once did. Current leading organists in the United States would include Frederick Swann, Thomas Murray, Diane Bish, Mickey Thomas Terry, Carlo Curley, Dan Miller, Carol Williams, and Felix Hell. This list is by no means all-inclusive; there are many fine organists throughout the country who either serve churches or are engaged in touring careers.

With these great organists in mind, there is a diversity of styles in playing the organ and the interpretation of the great organ works. E. Power Biggs and Virgil Fox represented two different schools of thought related to playing the organ. If you ask ten different organists how the organ should be played, you may get ten different answers. Some like tracker instruments, some prefer electro-pneumatic, some prefer loud organ music, some soft, some always use tremulants, some never, and there is no real absolute.

Certainly, cultural backgrounds play a part in the music, as does the denominational affiliation. The organ music found in a New England Episcopal parish, an African American Baptist church, a Jewish Synagogue, a Southern Baptist church, and New York Catholic Cathedral may be entirely different. The organists in churches of these traditions and faiths may play a vastly different repertoire of hymns, anthems and liturgical music. They may not have a repertoire of the major classical organ works, and may not understand the intricacies of organ registration.

Many churches today have a difficult time finding a trained organist whose salary expectations fit into their budget. In reality, most people who are hired to play organs for churches may not be trained specifically to play the organ. These musicians who play the organ may have a limited skill level. These organists may not play alternate arrangements of hymns, use an interlude between verses, alternate harmonization on the last verse, or trumpet solo voice on the melody or descant to add variety to their music. However, many resources are available that are music supplements for nonprofessionally trained organists. Both the Church Organ System and Allen Organs websites contain resource material that could benefit these musicians who play the organ. Such resources include registration guides and a CD-ROM based interactive instructional program by the Allen company. However, churches should consider contacting local college or university music departments as well as local chapters of the American Guild of Organists to identify musicians who could assist their music department.

CHAPTER 3:

The Development of the Organ in the 20th Century

𝒯o understand the current state of the pipe and digital organ industry, it is useful to review the history of the organ over the past century. In doing so, much can be learned about the major pipe and electronic organ companies. This information will be useful in assisting the organ committee in differentiating between organ companies and the instruments they produce. By understanding the trends in the organ industry, the committee may be better able to determine which company may be able to meet their current and long-term needs.

The Pipe Organ in the 20th Century

The pipe organ industry in the United States flourished in the late 1800's and early 1900's as major cities continued to expand and profit from the industrial revolution. This revolution allowed many churches across the country to invest in pipe organs as the main instrument for their sanctuaries. By 1910, many pipe organ companies were in operation in America including Hook and Hastings, Kimball, E.M. Skinner, Aeolian, M.P. Moller, Reuter, Kilgen, Wicks, Schantz and Austin. Many of their organs from the early 1900's are still in service today. All of these companies suffered from the great stock market crash of 1929 and the Great Depression. As a result, many changes took place, such as the acquisition of the Aeolian Organ Company by E.M. Skinner in January, 1932 to form the Aeolian-Skinner Organ Company. Many companies did not survive the economic turmoil, including Hook and Hastings, and Kimball.[1]

The Schantz Organ Company was founded in 1893 by A.J. Schantz in Orville, OH. The company is the oldest in the U.S. to remain in business and continued operation by the original family. Schantz did not attempt to replicate any style of organ building. Their focus was more on building a quality instrument than in creating a niche. Their instruments were well suited for many houses of worship across the country and employed electro-pneumatic controls. The largest Schantz organ is the four-manual 118 rank pipe organ at First Baptist Church in Orlando, FL. Abyssinian Baptist Church in New York City also purchased a five-manual 64 rank Schantz in the mid-1980's. The Schantz company was also contracted to conduct the restoration of the 1930's E.M. Skinner pipe organ of the Cleveland Civic Center.[2]

The M.P. Moller Organ Company was founded in Hagerstown, MD by Mathias P. Moller in 1881. M.P. Moller became the largest pipe organ company in America in the early 1900's. By 1920, Moller had built 3,000 organs, which had grown to 10,000 by the 1960's. Their many notable installations include the 103 rank Naval Academy Chapel organ, the 205 rank organ at Calvary Baptist Church in Charlotte, NC, the 213 rank West Point Cadet Chapel organ, the console of the 346 rank First Congregational Church of Los Angeles (arguably the largest church organ in the world), the five-manual console at the Crystal Cathedral in Garden Grove, CA, and the Longwood Gardens organ in San Diego, CA.[3] Similar to Schantz, Moller built electro-pneumatic organs and did not adhere to the tenets of any particular school of organ building. Unfortunately, the Moller Organ Company went out of business in 1992.

Austin Organs, Inc. is one of the last of the major organ companies of the early 20th century to remain in business. Originally founded in the 1800s by John and Basil Austin as the Austin Pipe Organ Company, the company was taken over by a second generation of Austin's in 1935. By 1924, the company had built over 1300 organs: 1 five-manual organ, 108 four-manual organs and 6 organs with over 100 stops. The company's instruments were known for their mechanical excellence and reliability. Of 48 patents in the early history of the company, probably the most well known was the Universal Air Chest, which provided steady wind supply for the pipes. Austin also was known for their unique console, which had stop tabs above the keyboards instead of drawknobs. This efficiency of design kept the stop controls in the line of sight of the organist, and made the console much smaller. A description of a tour to the Austin factory in Hartford, CT, is found later in the book.[4]

Figure 3 Three-Manual Austin Organ Console
(Shepherd of the Seas Chapel, Groton, CT)

The E.M. Skinner Organ company was founded by Earnest M. Skinner in 1903, who furthered the orchestral school of organ building. Mr. Skinner's organs were identified by plentiful 8' stops, few mixtures and mutation stops, and many orchestral voices. Stops attributed to E. M. Skinner include Erzahler (German for 'story-teller'), Orchestral Oboe, English Horn, French Horn, Klein Erzahler, Gross Gedeckt, Corno di Bassetto, Tuba Mirabilis, French

Trumpet, Orchestral Bassoon (16'), Gamba Celeste, Bombarde (32') and Violone (32').[5]   The Skinner 32' Bombarde was constructed of wood instead of metal and had a different tonal quality than the metal stop with traditional reed pipe components. E.M. Skinner was also known for his technological developments such as electro-pneumatic Swell shade controls and electro-pneumatic control of valves isolating organ pipes.[6] In the 1930's, G. Donald Harrison became the tonal director of the Skinner company, and brought a revolutionary approach to organ tonal design and voicing. His philosophy was to build organs that were capable of rendering music from every period of organ literature, to include German Baroque, French Romantic, and 20th century American.[7] This new organ was referred to as the "American Classic Organ," which characterized many of the organs built by the Aeolian-Skinner Company. As a result of Harrison's growing influence, E. M. Skinner left the company in 1935. Notable organs built by the Aeolian-Skinner Company and influenced by Mr. Harrison include those at the Groton School in Groton, MA, The Church of the Advent in Boston, the Mormon Tabernacle Organ of Salt Lake City, UT and the Trinity Church organ of Boston, MA.[8]

Figure 4 Four-Manual Aeolian-Skinner Organ Console
(National Cathedral, Washington, DC)

Walter Holtkamp was probably one of the most revolutionary organ builders of the 20th century aside from G. Donald Harrison. Even more radical than Harrison in opposition to the orchestral and baroque organs, Holtkamp felt that drastic changes were required. Most of his organs had completely exposed pipes and only the Swell was under expression. The Swell shades themselves were quite visible as well in Holtkamp organs.[9] He was extremely selective in the repertoire that he felt his organs should be used to play. Disproving of the romantic works, his organs were not capable of rendering music characteristic of the romantic period.

Charles Brenton Fisk took American organ reform to yet another level. He founded the C.B. Fisk Organ Company in Glouchester, MA, in 1961 after having worked previously for Holtkamp. Fisk organs were revolutionary in that they were mechanical action (tracker) organs. Instead of using electro-pneumatic controls, Fisk returned to the direct mechanical controls that were found in European organs of the Baroque period. These instruments were particularly useful for the authentic rendering of J.S. Bach and other Baroque composers. One of Fisk's first major works was a tracker organ at the Memorial Chapel at Harvard Unversity in 1967. This four-manual organ replaced the chapel's Aeolian-Skinner instrument of the 1930's. Fisk also built instruments for other academic institutions to include Stanford, Mt. Holyoke, SMU, Michigan, SUNY Buffalo and Oberlin College. The Oberlin organ at Finney Chapel (Opus 46) was, in fact, a mechanical action organ built in the symphonic style to replicate the work of French organbuilder Cavaille-Coll.[10]

Following the death of C.B. Fisk in 1983, the company undertook another challenge in 1992 with the completion of the Lay Family Concert organ (Opus 100) in Dallas' Myerson Symphony Hall. This eclectic organ is comprised of German Great and Positiv, French Swell and an English Tuba division, which give it a commanding presence over full orchestra. The crowning work of the Fisk company may be its grand organ at the Cathedral of Lausanne, Switzerland (Opus 120). This organ is a five-manual instrument of over 100 stops and was completed in 2003.[11] Although Fisk seems to have become more adventurous in organ building, the company appears to be committed to constructing mechanical action instruments that are particularly well suited for academic institutions and concert halls.

After the demise of the Moller company in 1992, several other companies were born of the ashes. Eastern Organ Pipes of Hagerstown maintained the former pipe construction business. The Full Organ Console Design focuses on CAD-design of organ consoles, modeled after M.P. Moller and Aeolian-Skinner consoles. The Allen Organ Company bought the rights to the Moller name and builds custom consoles in the Moller tradition. Moller was affected by the recession of the early 1990's in the same way that many organ companies were affected by the Great Depression of 1926.[12]

Similar to Moller, the Aeolian-Skinner Company lives on in several different ways. The Rodgers Instrument Corporation has archived many of the drawings from Aeolian-Skinner and incorporates their console design in the Rodgers consoles. Rodgers also models their digital organs tonally after the Aeolian-Skinner sound. Walker Technical Company, which will be spoken more of later, bought the rights to the name Aeolian-Skinner and specializes in digital extensions to pipe organs drawn from Aeolian-Skinner pipe samples. Additionally, the Robert M. Turner Organ Company builds custom organ consoles and models their designs after Aeolian-Skinner consoles.[13]

As the pipe organ industry peaked and waned in the 20th century, the world of the electronic organ was born in the early 20th century. The utility of the electronic organ has expanded tremendously as the technology improves at a rapid pace. Today's electronic organs are nearly indistinguishable from their pipe counterparts, and in many cases, occupy the same sound space.

Technological Developments and the Development of the Organ

Technological developments in the 20th Century have been astounding. With the Industrial Age in full force, many industries capitalized on inventions of the late 1800's, to include the invention of the light bulb by Thomas Edison. His pioneering work was not only to transform society, but the technology that would impact musical instruments as well. Early electronic organs were built based on basic electrical technology. Early organs produced pipe like tones using tone wheels or vacuum tubes in the 1930's and 40's. As the transistor was developed, they were incorporated into electronic organs in the 1950's. Because of solid state technology, analog organs in the 1960's were able to more closely approximate the pipe organ tone than their predecessors. However, the most significant improvements have been made with the coming of the Digital Age, which started in the early 1970's. As we enter the 21st Century, digital technology has allowed pipe organs to be sampled or simulated with amazing similarity. The current technology of the digital organs produces tonal qualities that are similar to wind-blown pipes. Many organs built today are in fact hybrid instruments: some of the voices are digitally sampled and some come from windblown pipes.

The Hammond Organ-Laurens Hammond

The Hammond organ was the first major electronic organ to be invented in the 20th century. Laurens Hammond invented the organ using his experience with electronics and his knowledge of the intricacies of watch-making. Laurens Hammond invented a tone wheel generator in 1934, which turned electrical wave patterns of alternating current into sound waves. By varying the speeds at which the tone wheels revolved, different notes could be produced. Different organ tones were produced by manipulating drawbars, which control the strength of the fundamental tones and overtones. The Hammond organ is comprised of two manuals of 61 notes each and a 25 note Pedal board. There are 36 drawbars to control the organ tones, with two sets of nine for each manual. Additionally, there are two drawbars for foot Pedals to control the 8' and 16' organ tones. The vibrato function was eventually developed, as was the use of the Leslie speakers. The combination of the Hammond organ and Leslie speaker creates the unforgettable sound of the instrument.[14] Hammond's original claim was that the Hammond organ sounded as good as a pipe organ.[15]

Figure 5: Hammond Organ B-3.
(Union Memorial United Methodist Church, St. Louis, MO)

The Hammond organ was accepted with much enthusiasm. Initial proponents included Henry Ford, George Gershwin and Ethel Smith. Hammonds were used extensively during World War II to provide religious and entertainment functions for the military. Largely used in gospel and popular music, it was not designed to be a direct competitor of the pipe organ. The Hammond B-3 organ has been legendary as a mainstay of the gospel, blues, jazz and even rock music genres. This organ was made popular by such greats as Jimmy Smith and Bill Doggett. There has been no attempt or desire to make the Hammond like a pipe organ; it creates a sound of its own and will be forever unique in that way. Nothing is more synonymous with early gospel music or blues than the Hammond B-3.

Allen Organ Company-Jerome Markowitz

Jerome Markowitz also pioneered the electronic organ industry. In 1937, he established the Allen Organ Company in Allentown, PA. As the first true competitor to the pipe organ, the Allen organ encountered many skeptics who were pipe organ purists. However, the electronic organ was a great challenge to the more costly pipe organ. The history of the Allen Organ Company is catalogued in Mr. Markowitz's work <u>Trials and Triumphs of an Organ Builder</u>, which gives excellent insight into his struggles in the development of the electronic organ. Mr. Markowitz possessed a strong background in electronics. Additionally, he leveraged the community of Pennsylvanian dutch craftsmen to start his company. He did so in a way completely different from Laurens Hammond, having sought to compete directly with the pipe organ in the institutional organ market. He felt that he could build a better, more capable organ that any pipe organ builder and avoid many of the shortcomings of the more costly instruments.

Initially, Allen's electronic organs produced sound through the use of vacuum tube tone generators. These oscillators produced the organ sound by simulating the harmonic structure of the sound produced by various organ stops. There was an obvious difference in the sound produced by the pipe organ and the early electronic equivalent, but the first steps had been made by Mr. Markowitz. Allen produced the first transistorized organs in 1958, replacing the bulky vacuum tubes. The first digital organ was developed and presented in 1971 from an alliance between the Allen Organ Company and North American Rockwell Corporation. Large Scale Integration (LSI) circuits now replaced simple transistors, and contained thousands of transistor circuits on one small piece of silicon. Ralph Deutsch was the technological genius behind the development of the digital tone generating system. In the ensuing years, much legal wrangling took place between the Allen Organ Company and many of their competitors, as everyone was anxious to capitalize on the technological advancements of the digital world.[16]

Figure 6 Four-Manual Allen Renaissance Organ.
(Allen Organ Company, Macungie, PA)

From the beginning, the Allen Organ Company has excelled in the area of building organs to the customers desires. In the 1940's, they built the first three-manual electronic organ simply because a customer wanted one. Today, an organist can choose from a wide selection of pipe samples to create a custom stop list, as well as any console design features desired. Allen has built on their years of experience in the digital sampling field. As a result, the company has compiled the most complete library of pipe organ sounds available. Noted concert organist Carlo Curley, largely regarded as having taken up the mantle from the late Virgil Fox, has called Allen "the archivist of the organ world." Allen Organs has probably built more custom five-manual organs than any other electronic organ builder. Installed in 2001, the custom five-manual organ at Bellevue Baptist Church in Cordova, TN, is the largest digital organ in the world boasting of over 380 stops. Additionally, Allen has built digital organs in the style of the French organ maker Cavaille-Coll both in console style and stop list. Allen has also recently embarked on many combination instrument projects, although once adverse to the combination pipe/electronic organ.

Rodgers Organ Company - Fred Tinker and Rodgers Jenkins

The Rodgers Organ Company was founded in 1958 by Fred Tinker and Rodgers Jenkins with the assistance of the Tektronic Company. Tektronic had originally turned down their business plan in 1957. The Rodgers Company was initially focused on the development of the first transistorized electronic organ and had totally transistorized their organs by 1962. Rodgers also moved into the realm of digital technology in the early 1970's. Whether Rodgers or Allen produced the first, or first musically successful, digital organ could be debated endlessly. In any case, early digital instruments sounds may not have been as convincing as some of the latest analog instruments in the early 1970's. At that time as well, Rodgers began production of combination instruments. Many of these instruments featured real principal or flute pipe ranks with electronic reeds and strings. Rodgers felt that the electronic principal sound at that time was not quite as convincing as real pipes. Rodgers chose another path in 1971 when they became the first electronic organ company to represent and sell pipe organs, with the Fratelli Ruffatti company of Padua, Italy.

During this period, Rodgers developed a relationship with well-known organist Virgil Fox, building the "Black Beauty" touring organ for him in 1968. In 1974, Fox dedicated the Rodgers five-manual organ in Carnegie Hall, the first five-manual electronic organ in the world. The Carnegie Hall organ was largely influenced by the five-manual Aeolian Skinner at Riverside Church where Virgil Fox presided for many years. The second five-manual electronic organ, the Rodgers "Royal V" was also used by Fox as his touring organ in 1975. By the early 1980's Rodgers produced small pipe/electronic organs for home or practice and became the first company to use microprocessors. By the late 1980's, Rodgers had added MIDI capability to all of their organs, built the five-manual 192 rank pipe organ for Second Baptist Church in Houston, and built their 1000th electronic organ with pipes.

Figure 7 Four-Manual Rodgers Console
(Sligo Seventh Day Adventist Church, Tacoma Park, MD)

Rodgers introduced the first stage of Parallel Digital Imaging (PDI) technology in 1990, in which microprocessors were used to recreate the sound of organ pipes. Using multi-point interpolation, Rodgers strove to represent the true sound of organ pipes with amazing clarity. The PDI technology also allowed the organs to achieve a tremendous richness of ensemble sound. During this time Rodgers also continued to build complete pipe organs, which was a rarity among electronic organ companies. After several generations of PDI organs, Rodgers introduced the Trillium organ series in 1999 which incorporated the ability to adjust the acoustics of the organ in any room setting. Now part of the Roland Instrument Corporation, Rodgers leveraged the research and development strength of this large company. This led to the application of the Rodgers/Roland RSS modeling system in the Trillium organs. Showing commitment to combination instruments in 2000, Rodgers built their 3000th electronic organ with pipes.[17]

Roland Instrument Corporation-Ikutaro Kakehashi

The discussion of electronic instruments would not be complete without mentioning the contributions of Ikutaro Kakehashi, the founder of the Roland Instrument Corporation. Mr. Kakehaski was born in Japan in 1930 and grew up in Osaka during the years following World War II. In his late teens, he started a watch repair shop. After facing a life threatening bout with tuberculosis, he used his self-acquired knowledge of electronics to start "Kakehashi Musen," an electric appliance shop in Osaka. Similar to Laurens Hammond, his experience with the precise machinery found in watches was instrumental in his success in the musical instrument industry. As the focus shifted to retail sales of electric appliances, he changed the name to Ace Electronic. Mr. Kakehashi continued to pursue his interest in electronic musical instruments.[18]

ACE Electronic Industries, Inc. was famed for its Rhythm Ace model R-1, a percussion instrument machine, and eventually became involved with the Hammond Organ Company (HOC) and Hammond International. While HOC built and sold organs in the United States, Hammond International built organs in Japan and marketed them in Asia. In 1968, Mr. Kakehashi formed a joint company between Ace Electronics and the Hammond International. With Mr. Kakehashi at its helm, the newly created company became known as Hammond International Japan (HIJ). HIJ pursued development of the tone wheel sound based on electronics. The Acetone GT-7 was the first electronic organ to produce a sine-wave (tone wheel) tone and was manufactured by HIJ. Mr. Kakehashi resigned from HIJ in 1972 and founded the Roland Instrument Corporation one month later.[19]

Roland capitalized on Mr. Kakehashi's years of experience in the electronic music industry. The company pioneered the area of synthesizers and was instrumental in the development of MIDI in the early 1980's (to be discussed later in this book). Mr. Kakehashi emphasized the importance of research and development in maintaining technical superiority over other companies, both in the keyboard, guitar and home organ markets. Roland developed several "tone wheel" organs using integrated circuit technology as opposed to the tone wheel generators of the Hammond organ. This was found to be a more cost effective means of sound generation. As a result, Hammond ceased production of the B-3 in 1972 due to its financial inefficiency. The electronic music industry was driven by the economy of the sound source. In 1973, Roland marketed the VK-6 and VK-9, combination organs with drawbars. Currently, Roland offers the VK-7 and VK-77 using virtual tone wheel technology. Ironically, Mr. Kakehashi turned down a merger proposal from the Hammond Organ Company in 1972.[20]

In 30 years of business, Roland has formed 23 joint venture companies around the world, beginning with Roland Australia in 1976. In 1988, Roland further diversified by acquiring the Rodgers Organ Company from Steinway Musical Properties of Boston. Rodgers has benefited greatly from the relationship because of Roland's strong emphasis on research and development, and Roland has diversified itself in the field of electronic instruments. For example, the RSS (Roland Sound Space) reverberation system was used in 1999 to compare a Rodgers digital organ to a pipe organ installed in a concert hall. The experiment demonstrated that both instruments were indistinguishable in the common environment of the concert hall, due to the quality of the Rodgers organ and the RSS system.[21]

Today's Opportunities for Flexibility

Over the past 30 years, great advances have been made in the realm of digital organ technology largely due to the work of the Rodgers and Allen Organ Companies. Because of these advances, churches now have a viable alternative to the pipe organ. A small pipe organ may cost $200,000 and a fairly large four-manual instrument may cost as much as $1,000,000 or more. In addition to the financial limitations, some churches or worship centers may not have sufficient space to install and maintain a pipe organ.

Currently the digital technology allows organ companies to digitally sample real pipes at a sampling rate, approximately 48 kHz (kilohertz), which is equivalent to or better than compact disk quality. This becomes the modern day tone generation system as real pipe sounds are literally recorded and played back. The various organ companies have different approaches to how they produce the sound and try to approximate the pipe organ.

While the pipe organ has not been completely reproduced, the digital organ provides an economic alternative to the pipe organ, at least in the short term. Although the pipe organ is initially more expensive, if properly maintained, it can be in service for hundreds of years. Because of technological improvements, most electronic organs seem to be replaced every 20-30 years if not sooner. Therefore, over a century, a church may have purchased two to four electronic organs. These purchases may result in the church paying the equivalent of the investment required to build one pipe organ and maintain it.

Today's technological advancements have also provided a compromise. Most digital organ builders can now be interfaced with real pipes. Similarly, most pipe organ companies are now incorporating digital voices into their instruments to replace the more expensive stops such as Reeds and 32' Pedal voices. These options allow churches to have an instrument whose core is real pipes, but the economy of using digital voices makes possible a much more capable and diverse instrument. The organ purists, including trained organists and pipe organ builders, have traditionally frowned upon the electronic alternatives. However, with recent improvements in sound quality, most objective people will take note of the progress that has been made in electronic organs.

This brings about an interesting dilemma. Real pipe organ builders have had to compete for centuries. The digital organ industry seems to be even more competitive. There is definitely a strong competition between representatives of the various electronic organ firms. Each is convinced that he has the most realistic pipe organ sound, and that the features they offer make their products head and shoulders above the competition. As technological advancements continue, we may reach a plateau, a point at which it is impossible to more closely approximate the pipe organ. Because of the difference in the way that pipe organs and their electronic counterparts produce sounds, the full richness of the pipe organ may not be fully recreated.

The Hammond Organ Today

The Hammond organ has now come into a new era. Hammond organs built today incorporate digital technology in their tone generation. The old tone wheel generation has been replaced by digital samples. The Suzuki Company now owns the company. Partially because of this new partnership, Hammond has recently embarked into the world of the classical organ, also featuring digital pipe samples. As a result, they now offer a hybrid organ that combines the traditional drawbars with traditional pipe organ voices.

Churches who have a strong use of gospel or contemporary music will most likely have a Hammond organ. If this is the dominant type of music, the church may exclusively use this type of organ and piano to accompany the choirs, for hymns and for other worship music. The Hammond drawbars allow the fundamental organ tones to be mixed with overtones and produce a virtually unlimited combination of sounds. Tens of thousands of individual tones can be produced by the different combinations of drawbars.

The Hammond has an unmistakable sound and is an instrument all of its own. It does not seek to directly recreate the pipe organ, nor can a pipe organ simulate its unique sound. The original Hammond is also a bit different from the modern organs, which use digital samples instead of the vintage tone wheel generation. As a digital pipe organ cannot completely recreate the pipe organ sound, the same is true for the new digital Hammonds. The Hammond organ can be a relatively inexpensive addition to a church's music program. This type of organ is noted for its quick response and ability to screech and whine like no other instrument. Therefore, it is particularly useful in gospel and contemporary music. It is not meant, however, to render much classical organ literature, especially when compared to the digital pipe organ. However, the Hammond Suzuki Organ Company now produces a hybrid tone-wheel/classical organ that allows the flexibility of playing many types of music.

The Hammond Suzuki company is also developing a line of classical organs. Built in Holland, these "Concert Series" organs come in both two and three-manual models and have traditional organ stops. The pricing is as much as 60% less than comparative models from the major organ companies, and may be a suitable option for smaller churches.

Several other companies are also producing "tone wheel" organs. As mentioned before, the Roland Instrument Corporation has been producing "tone wheel" organs for many years. Currently, Roland markets the VK-77 and VK-7 instruments, both of which are portable. Rather than use the Leslie speaker, by using "virtual tone-wheel" technology, a fairly standard speaker can be used and still generate the "Hammond" effect. Additionally, the Viscount company (part of Church Organ Systems) is marketing the DB-25 and OB-5 "tone wheel" organs.

The Contemporary Organist/Musician

The contemporary church has seen a tremendous change in worship styles. Many evangelical or nondenominational churches have embraced music which is similar to current popular music from rhythm and blues, rock and jazz to gospel. The traditional hymnal is not used and the lyrics to worship songs are seen on large video screens. Along with the change in music styles has come a change in instruments used in worship. The Hammond organ has become much more popular in non liturgical worship settings accompany the music. Along with the Hammond, the contemporary keyboard has become very popular. Along with these new instruments has come a new breed of musicians who are more versed in contemporary worship and praise music than the more traditional repertoire.

The musician may be more of a keyboardist than an organist in the purest sense, because of these changes mentioned above. Many of these musicians may have had formal training in piano and may play by ear. Although the ability to play the Hammond organ may usually come by listening to others play, there are very few formal settings to learn how to play the instrument. However, there are many resources that contain excellent opportunities to develop skills in playing the Hammond. The book <u>Beauty in the B: A Guide</u>

to the Hammond Organ contains excellent playing tips and other useful reference material. Other sources of information and training include the Wheatworks website, the Gospel Music Convention of America, and the Hampton Minister's Conference and Organists' and Choir Guild Conference (HMC/OCG). The HMC/OCG offers workshops for both traditional pipe organists and Hammond organ organists, recognizing that both instruments are widely used in African American worship settings.

With the discussions of traditional organists, Hammond organists and keyboardists in mind, one must be very specific when discussing the capabilities of a musician. Just because someone is an "organist" does not mean that they necessarily are capable of playing an pipe organ and a Hammond organ. Although both are essentially organs, there is a specific style of playing characteristic of both instruments. Additionally, a pianist may not be able to play either type of organ. This presents a potential problem for churches in search of a new organ or an new musician.

Churches must understand clearly the capabilities of the musicians that they hire and their willingness to receive additional training to develop their skills. The American Guild of Organists has a fine program that specifies the qualification level of musicians and the expected compensation for their level of training. However, this is not the case for most musicians who may not be a member of a formal guild. If a church has a pipe organ but is only able to find a musician who is experienced in the Hammond organ, they may find the pipe organ sitting silent. Similarly, a musician with formal pipe organ training would most likely be unsatisfied at a church that only has a Hammond organ. Many churches avoid this dilemma by having multiple instruments and multiple musicians. There are few organists who can play pipe organs and Hammond organs equally well because the technique required to adequately play a pipe organ and a Hammond are radically different. Many churches have fine pipe or digital organs sitting idle because the musician they are able to hire is not trained to play the instrument and is not willing to learn. This paradox is discussed in depth in Dr. Abbington's Let Mt. Zion Rejoice!.

CHAPTER 4

Organan Technology

*D*igital organ companies are protective of their technological secrets. Many of the developments and inventions made by organ companies have been patented. For obvious reasons, these companies are reluctant to fully explain the technologies that are used in their organs in promotional literature. The informational brochures provided by digital organ companies are descriptive of their instruments, but the information is general in nature. Without having studied the organ and having an electrical engineering degree, much of the technical information may be very hard for organ committee members to understand. This chapter is written to explain the major components of electronic organs. Some of the capabilities of contemporary organs are explained, as well as some of the options that are available to upgrade a traditional pipe organ.

Sound Generator Systems

The world of the digital organ has changed due to the advances of digital technology. The science of tone generation has changed appreciably. From vacuum tubes to transistor tone generators, the digital revolution allowed large scale integrated (LSI) circuits to create the sounds that are produced by the organ. These newer technologies are also more cost effective than technologies of the past. For example, using the tone wheel generators became cost prohibitive and eventually forced the Hammond Company to stop production of their famed B-3 organ in the early 1970's. The technological advances of today are centered on digital sampling of real pipe organs. The organ voices are digitally recorded and then played back through the organ system. Every nuance of the pipe's sound can be captured due to the high sampling rate available through digital technology. Some companies boast a high sampling rate that exceeds CD quality, with a standard data rate of 48 kHz. The fact that electronic organs are using real pipes as a standard is a testament to the superiority of the pipe organ. However, the digital mastery makes the reproduction of sound much less costly. A very capable digital instrument can be built for significantly less than its pipe equivalent because of the relative cost of an electronic instrument and the advances of digital technology. The ability to sample any pipe voice gives the flexibility of recreating virtually any pipe organ tonal style.

The Rodgers Corporation does offer a technology that allows sounds to be blended in a parallel manner through computers and produces a stereophonic output. The proprietary Parallel Digital Imaging, developed in 1991, allows Rodgers to combine the various notes and stops being played simultaneously using powerful 486 kHz (kilohertz) processors. Each note of every stop has two digital samples for stereophonic output, and is controlled using the microprocessors and software controls. The stereophonic (left, right and bass) output allows the combined sound of the organ to be amplified and played through the speakers. Other digital organ companies divide the sound production by organ division (Great or Swell) or by stop type (principal, string, etc.). As part of the multi-million dollar Roland Group since 1988, the Rodgers Corporation leverages the research and development capability of this pioneer in the digital music industry to stay on the cutting edge of digital organ technology.[1]

Hammond organs built today use digital samples of tone wheel sounds rather than the vintage tone wheel generators. Similar to the digital pipe organs, the sampled Hammond sound is not quite the same as the vintage tone wheel sound. There are several hybrid tone wheel/classical organs available today because of the digital sampling technology. Hammond Suzuki has produced the 926 Classic organ. This organ features drawbars and traditional pipe sounds on the Swell, Great and Pedal as well as MIDI voices. For several years, Rodgers produced the W-5000, a similar instrument, which has been discontinued in favor of the VK-77 praise combo. The VK-77 has the added flexibility of being portable. These organs would be great choices for churches that want a contemporary sound but need traditional sounds. In the case of these hybrid organs, the tone wheel and pipe sounds area available without buying a separate organ.

Amplifiers and Speaker Systems

In addition to the sound generation system, electronic organs use amplifiers and speakers to actually amplify and project the sound. Unlike pipe organs in which the sound generator and the amplifier are all contained within each pipe, electronic organs must fuse these very distinct components to produce and project the organ sound. Amplifiers are used to increase the intensity of the sound signal produced by the digital sound generator. Most amplifiers are contained in cabinets external to the organ console. The amount of power produced by the amplifier is normally given in units of watts of power. The signal is now strong enough to be projected through special speakers specifically designed for organs. Usually, several types of speakers are used. For the manuals, moderately sized speakers that approximate the size of home stereo speakers are used. Large pedal cabinets as big as a foot locker are often used for the low frequency sound produced by pedal sounds. Sound output of the organ is also divided into discrete channels. A small two-manual organ may have only a few channels, one for each manual and another for the pedals at several hundred watts of power. Large three and four-manual organs may have between 10 and 30 channels at almost 3000 watts of power.

The first revolutionary speaker was the Gyrophonic Projector developed by the Allen Organ Company in 1949. The projector was used to "liven" the sound of the early electronic organ and make it sound more "pipelike." The speaker assembly was turned by a simple AC motor which could be turned on and off by the organist. Next to be developed was the Leslie speaker which augmented the sound of the Hammond organ in the 1960's. Invented by Don Leslie, the Leslie speaker has variable speed rotating speaker horns that give the Hammond sound a vibrato effect. Mr. Leslie was originally trying to make the Hammond have more of a theater pipe organ sound by varying the directional output of the speakers. In actuality, he produced an effect that has become a vital part of the Hammond sound, especially in jazz and gospel music.[2]

Today's advanced speaker technology focuses on the frequency range of sound and the type of sounds being projected. "Tweeters" are used for higher frequency ranges, mid-range frequency drivers and "woofers" for low frequencies round out the spectrum. Sub woofers add extra foundation to the pedal stops, and are built for the extremely low frequencies.

Rodgers "Audiophile" speakers are designed for these specific frequency ranges. Rodgers also incorporates speakers that are designed for reed voices such as Festival Trumpet or Tuba. Bi-amplification is also used in Rodgers organs to improve the performance of the speakers. The low frequency signal for the sub woofer is separated from the mid-range and high frequency signal and separately amplified to a higher wattage. The sub woofers have a 15" cone driver and have a frequency range from 16 Hz to 100 Hz. Therefore, mid-range and high frequency drivers do not amplify very low frequency signals and sub woofers don't amplify higher frequency signals.[3]

Allen's "Herald" loudspeakers incorporate a Trumpeteer Wave Projector which is designed to accommodate the transient response of the pipe sounds. These speakers have a frequency response from 40 Hz to 20 kHz. Allen also augments their organ speaker system with SR (Seismic Radiator) Series sub woofers. The speakers contain a custom designed 15" high-mass, super-low frequency, double magnet active driver and several passive radiators. The two models of the sub-woofers extend the low end frequency down to roughly 15 Hz, and require between 100 and 180 Watts of power. Allen's expertise in the area of speaker technology was greatly enhanced by their acquisition of Legacy Audio in 1996. Legacy was founded in 1983 by Bill Dudleson and focused in the area of high end loudspeakers.[4]

Added Digital Voices

The Walker Technical Company specializes in providing digital extensions to pipe organs. The Walker sound library includes E.M. Skinner and Aeolian-Skinner voices, and the company has rights to the name "Aeolian-Skinner." Their digital voices are particularly useful in expanding older E.M. Skinner or Aeolian-Skinner pipe organs, as both of these companies have been out of business for some time. Walker also manufactures speakers which are used in their pipe voice additions. Many older Rodgers and Allen organs have been configured with Walker Technical speakers. Since these other companies are marketing their own speakers for their organs, they do not actively endorse the use of Walker speakers with their organs. Walker also uses an auto tuning device with pipe organs that was one of the first such devices to be developed. Each division that contains Walker extension voices has sensors in that chamber (Great, Swell, Choir, etc.) that automatically tunes the digital voices to the pipe voices in that division.[5]

Acoustic Enhancement Systems

The technological advances of today also allow for the digital organ to transform an acoustically dead room into a highly reverberrant environment. The Allen Organ Company introduced a new acoustic enhancement program called 'Acoustic Portrait' in 2005. Allen has studied the reverberation conditions of several famous organ venues in Europe. From these studies, they have developed a system that recreates these acoustic properties using complex mathematical computations. Much more detail is provided on the technology behind this system on the Allen Organ website.[6]

The Rodgers Corporation developed a RSS (Roland Sound Sampling) Ambient Sound System. This allowed the organist to adjust the character of reverberation in the room. The Rodgers Corporation tested this system against a pipe organ installed in a concert hall in 1999. The test showed the digital organ's sound was "fully comparable" to the pipe organ.

Sound Generation and Reproduction

Most builders today use real pipe organ digital recordings or samples as the source of each of the pipe notes. Based on the sampling rate, the definition of each sample varies. Rodgers digitally combines the samples waveforms and outputs the sound stereophonically. Most builders playback the sounds from each voice which outputs through specific speaker channels. Allen offers an extensive sample library that allows an organist to select the specific stops that will be included on their organ. Most digital organ builders offer standard models that contain preselected stops. Many of these organs do contain a substantial number of second voices that incorporate stops from different schools of organ building. Most organ builders also allow each organ stop to be voiced much like a real pipe organ. The tonal characteristics of each stop can be adjusted as desired. In most organs, other percussive voices are available as well. These include the harp, chimes, handbells, and zimbelstern. Some organs also have choral voices, which have been derived from actual recordings of live choirs. These additional features can all be used in creative ways by the organist. These voices can also be augmented by the use of MIDI sound sequencers. As mentioned before, MIDI allows the organist to access hundreds of additional sounds to include trumpets, strings, drums and synthesizers. These systems in some cases allow the organs registration to be saved and an entire piece of music to be recorded. This affords the organist the opportunity to listen to his or her own music and critique their performance. They could also use this feature to enable them to direct a choir simultaneously. Most digital organs have some means of simulating the reverberation effect of a pipe organ in a huge cathedral. Even pipe organs can sound dead in some venues, especially in contemporary worship settings which contain carpet and other sound dampening material. These systems allow the organist to virtually recreate the acoustic setting that they wish to play in and to select the duration of the reverberation.

Control features: Organ Consoles

The organ console is the control station for the instrument. For tracker pipe organs, there is a mechanical link between the keys, the stops drawn and the air supply to corresponding pipes. Pipe organs using electro-pneumatic controls use electronic circuit boards in the console to control the air supply to pipes. In digital organ consoles, the sound generator circuit boards are also located in the console. Most larger digital organs have external speakers, while some smaller instruments have self-contained speakers.

Many organ consoles are constructed of a hard wood such as oak. The wood can be stained to match other wood work in the sanctuary. A standard light or dark stain is also available. Depending on the builder, consoles can be plain or have ornate wooden carving. Organ consoles typically have between two and five keyboards, although some only have one, and larger organs may have six or seven. The face of each key is attached to a key stick, which connects to relays for the corresponding note. Key sticks are constructed of wood or a combination of wood and plastic. The keyboards themselves can be fairly basic, with white naturals and black sharps. Some consoles have keys made of bone, ebony, maple, walnut or other exotic materials.

If the console has drawknob stop controls, these controls are located in stopjambs on either side of the keyboards. Most tilt tab (or stop tab) stop controls are located in rows above the keyboards. Mechanical (moving) or lighted drawknobs are found on most organs today. In the lighted capture system for drawknobs, the drawknob lights when pulled out and then springs back into place. Traditional pipe organs use moving drawknobs that can actually be pulled out when the stop is selected. The merits of each can be debated endlessly. Many organists use the organ presets to select the stop combinations they desire rather than individually selecting each stop. On the other hand, if the desire is to simulate the pipe organ, the moving controls may be more realistic. For instruments with moving drawknobs, different options are available for their color and design. The standard drawknob is black with a white face and black lettering. A variety of other combinations are also available, to include walnut, maple or all white drawknobs. Some stops are color coded to reflect the stop family: reeds are red, strings are green, flutes are blue and principals are black.

Above the keyboards is the coupler rail on a drawknob console. Couplers from each manual to the Pedal are normally at 8' pitch and are on the left. Inter manual couplers (Swell to Great) are also at 8' pitch. Intra-manual couplers (Swell to Swell 4' or Swell to Swell 16') are also included. These add pitches an octave above or below the normal pitch played for the manual to the unison pitch. If the 'unison-off' coupler is selected also, only voices above or below the octave of the key played will be heard. The music rack is located above the coupler rail. Most consoles have a clear plexiglass lighted music rack. These music racks also can be obtained in a wood lattice or solid wood and may have adjustments to raise or lower the height. A music rack light is a norm.

Beneath each keyboard are combination pistons. These pistons can be set for desired combinations of stops that can be selected by the organist. On the left side are located general combination pistons, usually the first five under the Great and the last five under the Swell. Towards the center are the divisional combination pistons for each manual. On the right are pistons for coupling the manuals to the Pedal or to other manuals. Some organs also have pistons for coupling MIDI to the manuals, bass or melody couplers, or vibrato. There is usually a cancel piston, which turns off all stops, and at least one Tutti piston for a full organ combination. For organs that have multiple memory levels, different organists can have their own memory level to set their desired combination.

Beneath the keyboards and above the pedal board are the expression pedals. A three-manual organ with a Choir division will have an expression pedal for the Choir, Swell and crescendo. Some organs also have an expression pedal for the Great/Pedal combination. On either side of the expression pedals are the toe studs for memory actuation. On the left are typically the toe studs for general combinations, and on the right are the studs for Pedal combinations, Tutti, zimbelstern, and reversible studs for 32' stops. The pedal board extends from the bottom of the console below the toe studs and expression pedals. The pedals on most pedal boards are concaved, although some smaller organs may have flat pedals.

One builder should be particularly noted for its emphasis on customization. The Allen Organ Company makes many custom features standard for many of its instruments. Of particular note, they have built numerous five-manual organs which are entirely customized. Most of these organs are found in large sanctuaries that seat up to 10,000 people. A pipe organ of the same dimension would no doubt cost several million dollars and take up an enormous amount of space. The utility of such large instruments is relatively limited. The Rodgers Organ Company makes all of their four-manual instruments to custom standards. In any case, most churches will be well served with either a two or three-manual instrument. The average church organist is probably not even capable of making use of the full resources of a four or five-manual instrument. For many, the resources of a three-manual instrument may not be fully utilized.

Used Organs

When a church is in need of a new organ, they may not consider used organs when embarking upon their search. One of the most prestigious organs in the United States is, in fact, comprised of new and used organ components. The Hazel Wright Organ at the Crystal Cathedral in Garden Grove, CA, includes pipes from the Aeolian-Skinner organ formerly of Lincoln Center. The current organ combines the Aeolian-Skinner organ, new Ruffatti pipes and digital voices by Walker. The console was constructed by the Ruffatti company and controls all of the organ's resources. Being the largest drawknob console in the world, the organ controls over 380 stops and has 66 coupler tabs. A second console was built in 1996 by the Moller company to control the organ during special pageants in the Cathedral.[7]

The Hazel Wright Organ was designed by the late organ virtuoso Virgil Fox. Although not installed at the time of his death, the organ is a lasting testimony of the genius of this fine musician. The Rodgers 'Royal V' was played for Mr. Fox's funeral at the Cathedral following his untimely death in 1980. The organ was made famous by the televised 'Hour of Power' broadcast and featured Dr. Frederick Swann as Cathedral organist. Dr. Swann presided at the great organ for 16 years and is now in a retired status. He currently serves as President of the American Guild of Organists and has a vibrant concert schedule. The Robert Tall Associates website features his Rodgers custom four-manual organ located in his California home: a 'smaller' sibling of the great Hazel Wright Organ.[8]

There are many resources available which offer information about used organs. Quite often, these used organ components are more affordable than new organ parts. Many websites list used organs for sale, organ pipes and other components. Such sites include: Organ Historical Society, Organ Clearing House, Keyboard Exchange, Keyboard Trader, Ebay, Marshall Ogletree, R.A. Daffer Organs, B-3 World and Allen Organs Wholesale. It is vitally important that a trained organ specialist determine if used organ pipes can be salvaged. Some older pipes can be reused, while others may no longer be tonally or musically acceptable.

A church could work with the lead organ company to formulate the many options that are suitable for its needs. A used organ is not necessarily very old. Several digital organs seen on used organ websites are five years old or newer. Some of these instruments were purchased by individuals who were forced to sell their instruments due to space considerations. One organ was being sold by a church that had decided to purchase a Hammond organ instead of the digital pipe organ they had purchased several years prior.

In order to augment a digital instrument, a church could find 5 to 30 ranks of used pipes from one of these resources. In fact, pipes themselves are timeless resources. They have been in use in some organs for hundreds of years. The limiting components, however, are the blower mechanism, pneumatic or mechanical action components, or the console itself. The pipes are rarely the limiting factor in the performance of an older pipe organ. With this in mind, a church could easily find a tremendous resource of used pipes that could be the foundation for a great combination pipe/digital instrument.

A good survey of used organs also illustrates an important fact about the value of various instruments. After viewing the organs being sold on the Organ Clearing House, Keyboard Trader and Ebay websites over several months, it is clear that pipe organs are a better long-term investment than their electronic counterparts. For example, a three-manual Aeolian-Skinner pipe organ Opus 1006A upgraded in 1954 was listed on the Organ Clearing House in 2005 for $100,000. This organ was probably built in the 1940's for about $40,000. Assuming 4% inflation, $40,000 in 1940 would be equivalent to over $200,000 in 2005 dollars. The value of an older pipe organ is a function of age, musicality and condition of pipes, tonal quality, reliability of pipe controls and condition of the console. Many older pipe organs may have maintained their value or even appreciated in value.

Unfortunately, the same cannot be said for electronic organs. Three-manual analog organs from the 1970's are being sold today for between $5000 and $12,000. The original sale price of these instruments was on the order of $30,000. Several organs have been offered recently on the Keyboard Trader website that are two years old or less. They are being sold at roughly 60% of the original sale price. One organ had been purchased two months prior to being listed and was being sold for a larger model. It also was being sold at a significantly reduced price. Buying an electronic organ today is, quite frankly, somewhat like buying a new car: it depreciates in value the minute you "drive it off the lot."[9]

The combination organ (pipes and electronic) is probably the best of both worlds. This option embraces the value and timelessness of real pipes, while leveraging the economy and quality of today's digital voices. The reality is that an all-pipe organ is not a financially viable option for most congregations. However, they are much more likely to be able to afford a combination instrument with the possibility of adding more pipe ranks in the future. Taking advantage of the resources available to locate used organs (both pipe and digital) can provide possible alternatives for those search of a new instrument.

In addition to having a need for additional organ pipes, a church may have a need to replace an outdated or worn organ console and pipe control system. These services may be provided by both the Allen and Rodgers companies who could also add digital voices to the organs. This option is based on the expertise of the local Allen or Rodgers organ representative. Most pipe organ companies will also provide these services, but there are several companies that specialize in designing and building organ consoles. In addition to building large organs of over 100 ranks, the Robert M. Turner company of California specializes in building consoles in the tradition of E.M. Skinner. Following the demise of the M.P. Moller Pipe Organ Company, it's console design arm still maintains a presence on the internet. Due to the expertise of D. G. Dauphinee, Moller became the premier builder of organ consoles and adopted computer drafting of organ consoles using AutoCAD. Moller's final project was the design of the second five-manual console for the Hazel Wright organ at the Crystal Cathedral, located in the balcony. Mr. Dauphinee still provides organ console design using computer aided drafting (CAD) technology. His console designs are made to authentically replicate consoles of E.M. Skinner, Aeolian-Skinner and M.P. Moller. The design then can be given to the organ company which would build the console. [10]

CHAPTER 5:

Pianos, Keyboards and MIDI

$\mathcal{A}$lthough the focus of the book is the organ, this chapter is devoted to looking at pianos and keyboards. This discussion will lead back to the organ through reviewing the development of Musical Instrument Digital Interface (MIDI), which is now incorporated on most organs today. Most churches will have some type of piano in addition to an organ. In reality, pianos and organs are both keyboard instruments and require similar technique to play. Modern technology has brought both instruments closer together. Many digital pianos contain both organ sounds and piano sounds. In fact, most organists have started their training with the piano because it allows fundamental keyboard techniques to be developed. Let us now look explore the world of the piano, keyboards and MIDI. This information will help understand how MIDI has been interfaced with organs of many types.

The piano is a stringed instrument that developed about 250 years ago from the harpsichord. The standard piano has one keyboard with 88 keys. When a key on the piano is depressed, the mechanism allows the corresponding hammer to hit the string of appropriate diameter and length for the desired pitch. A certain amount of force is required to overcome the resistance in the key to hammer mechanism and cause the hammer to strike its string. The strings are connected to the sound board and once struck, the vibration of the string produces the sound. The wooden piano case acts as an amplifier as well as containing the sound board and strings. Every component of the piano literally impacts the sound produced, because the entire piano vibrates once a string is struck by the hammers.

Pianos can be found in two basic types: upright and grand. The grand piano is normally between 5 feet and 9 feet in length, and its strings and sound board extend horizontally from the keyboard. These pianos are used mainly in concert halls, churches or other large venues, and some smaller grand pianos are found in homes. The top of the piano can be raised or kept closed in order to change the volume of sound and sound character of the piano. In the upright or spinet piano, the sound board is vertical and arranged almost perpendicular to the keyboard. These pianos are normally used as home or practice instruments.

In many ways, the piano is drastically different from the organ. The organ is capable of sustaining individual notes and even large chords. The dynamic range of the organ is also much wider than the piano and, with its many stop families, is capable of many different tone colors. A piano has either two or three foot pedals which control the volume of sound and allow chords and notes to be sustained. Techniques for playing the organ are also different from the piano. Piano keyboards are velocity sensitive in that the harder one strikes the keys, the louder the sound that is produced. The organ's keyboard does not control the loudness of the sound produced.

Two of the most widely known piano manufacturers are Steinway and Baldwin. The Steinway Piano Company was founded in 1853 by Henry Engelhart Steinway, a German immigrant. He pioneered the area of modern piano development and was a prolific inventor. Mr. Steinway held over 110 patents, many of which greatly affected the design of modern pianos. Today, Steinway only produces about 5,000 pianos worldwide annually. Although their cost is high, Steinway pianos are tremendous investments. According to the Steinway website, a Forbes Magazine estimates that the retail value of a Steinway concert grand will increase by over 200% in ten years. Many noted pianists are firm believers in the quality of sound produced by the Steinway, as well as the touch of their keyboards.[1]

The Baldwin Piano Company was founded in 1862 by Dwight Hamilton Baldwin. By 1913, Baldwin pianos were sold in over 30 countries. It represented an important advancement in piano design. Baldwin has diversified by making upright pianos, the Pianovelle digital piano, and the Concert Master player system. Baldwin pianos have always had an excellent reputation and continue to have a dominating presence in the piano market. Baldwin did not limit themselves to the piano market and introduced their first electronic organ in 1946. In 1965, the Baldwin SD10 concert grand piano was introduced.[2]

When synthesizers were developed in the 1970's, companies involved expanded the piano and added string, electric organ and other symphonic sounds. These early synthesizers contained closer to 60 keys, which did not have the weighted feel of the acoustic piano keyboards. Originally, it was not possible to play multiple sounds at one time and usually multiple keyboards could not be played together. The ability to layer sounds as in a pipe organ was impossible. Part of the problem was that different keyboard companies did not use the same digital format to control their keyboards. Additionally, few keyboards had the same list of sounds available. To say the least, configuration controls were not in place within the digital keyboard industry. But these keyboards introduced a contemporary sound to worship and went along with the music published by such companies as *Maranantha!*. Companies such as Kurzweil, Roland, Technics and Yamaha led the way in this industry. The problems of incompatibility of keyboards and lack of standardization were addressed with the creation of MIDI.[3]

The contemporary movement within the Christian church has seen the rising popularity of praise and worship music. In some churches, the "praise team" has replaced the choir and the "praise band" has replaced the pipe organ. In his best selling book, <u>The Purpose Driven Church</u>, Pastor Rick Warren of the Saddleback Community Church suggests the organ be replaced with a MIDI Band. Pastor Warren indicates that, "all you need is a MIDI keyboard and some MIDI discs."[4] To say the least, his feeling is that the pipe organ is a relic of the past and should be replaced by a more contemporary instrument. His point that most un-churched people will be reached by contemporary music is well taken. However, we are admonished to let everything praise the Lord, not

just contemporary instruments. Maybe you're not ready to disman-
tle all of the pipe organs and sell the pipes for scrap metal, but you
just want to know more about contemporary music and how to
liven up your church.

Musical Instrument Digital Interface (MIDI)

MIDI is a data transfer language that allows digital keyboards or
synthesizers to control each other. It also allows sound accessible in a
sound sequencer to be accessed by any MIDI compatible keyboard.
MIDI was developed in the early 1980's to standardize keyboards
and synthesizers and to create a common language that would allow
many keyboards to be interfaced together. Prior to MIDI, there was
no standard interface that allowed multiple keyboards to be played
together. Also, there was no standard order of sounds found in the
many keyboard that were available at the time.

The leading keyboard companies at that time came together to
develop not only the digital interface, but to standardize the voices
that were available in keyboards and sound sequencers. The companies involved were Kawai, Korg, Roland, Yamaha, Oberheim and
Sequential circuits. At a June 1981 meeting of the National
Association of Music Merchants (NAMM), they discussed the
initial framework of MIDI. By 1984, the detailed specification of
the music interface was finalized and made available for many
other companies.[5]

Today, a majority of keyboards are MIDI compatible. Most
digital organs are also designed to be interfaced with MIDI
sequencers. In fact, some pipe organs are built with MIDI compatibility, especially if they are augmented with digital voices. For
detailed information on MIDI, an excellent reference is <u>An
Introduction to the Creation of Electroacoustic Music</u> by Samuel
Pellman. This book uncovers the technical details not only of
MIDI, but gives the background on electroacoustic music as a
whole.

There are several key terms that must be understood in dealing
with MIDI. First is General MIDI. General MIDI is a set of technical specifications that guides the format of the MIDI signals. MIDI

is basically digital binary code that sends commands to or from keyboards or sequencers. The following is a set of typical MIDI commands: note on, note off, note volume, note sound and note velocity. GS MIDI is a format developed by the Roland Corporation that is a standard set of sounds. Music recorded in this format will therefore have the same sound when played back through another MIDI device.

Unlike a cassette recorder, MIDI is not a recording of sounds produced by a musical performance. MIDI represents the voices, tempo, sequence of notes, and volume that make up the music. Instead of projecting the sounds recorded by a musical device, when a MIDI recording is played back, it gives the commands to start and stop notes, the sound to use and the volume to the keyboard or organ to which the MIDI sequencer is connected. In this way, a MIDI recording is much more flexible than an aural recording. A MIDI recording allows you to change the tempo, add or change voices, layer tracks, or transpose the music to a different key. All of these manipulations can be performed by a MIDI sound sequencer.

MIDI devices have a standard set of connections: in, out and thru. The in connector is the input to the device from other MIDI devices. The out connector sends signals to other MIDI devices from the given MIDI component. The thru connector passes information from input received to the MIDI device to another MIDI instrument. MIDI keyboards and sequencers are connected through these ports using co-axial cable.

MIDI Sequencers

MIDI sound sequencers can be used to record musical performances and to augment an organ with additional voices that differ from the traditional organ sounds. The Rodgers PR-300S will be discussed to explain the resources of a MIDI sequencer and some of its capabilities. The PR-300S was upgraded in 2005 to the MX-200.

The PR-300S has the ability to access over 350 voices. There are 128 individual sounds accessible in this sequencer (such as the piano), some of which have up to 10 variations. All of the sounds are in accordance with the GS MIDI numbering sequence. The PR-300S allows MIDI voices to be played from Rodgers organs or other keyboards. Additionally, it allows several recording options. First, the organ alone can be recorded using the PR-300S. This may be useful if the organist is not available for a particular service, such as a wedding. All desired music for the service could be recorded and played later during the service. As a reminder, the MIDI sequencer does not record the sounds produced by the organ. It records the sequence and velocity of the notes played and the sounds that are selected on the organ in digital code. When "played back," the commands are given to the organ and the organ is "played" real-time by the sequencer just as originally played by the organist.

The PR-300S also allows multi-track sequencing. For example, five MIDI voices could be recorded individually on separate tracks, then layered over the organ recording to obtain unique effects. The sequencing feature and the recording feature are both contained within the PR-300S. The device is divided into 16 channels. Channels 1-9 are reserved for MIDI voices. Channel 10 is used for the drum kit. Channels 11-16 are reserved for the Rodgers organ. As different tracks are recorded individually and layered together, the PR-300 also allows the timing of each track to be coordinated because each track may not exactly be played at the same tempo.

Augmenting an organ with a sound sequencer gives the organist flexibility never allowed before on any instrument. From one "work station" the musician can select from over 350 different contemporary sounds and several drum kits. At the same time, the resources of the traditional pipe organ are also accessible. Instead of having a pipe organ for a traditional service and a series of keyboards for contemporary services, a sound sequencer such as the PR-300S allows a church to have an instrument capable of rendering any type of music through a high quality sound system. Organ consoles today are configured to play MIDI voices on each manual and on the pedals. Rodgers organs even have two MIDI channels per division available. Instead of having several keyboards stacked on top of each other with wires and cables connecting them in a maze of co-axial spaghetti, the organ in the MIDI mode can be transformed from a traditional pipe organ console to a contemporary music work station.[6]

CHAPTER 6:

The Organic Company

*O*rgan companies can be very different depending on the type of organ they build, whether it is pipe, electronic, tone wheel, or tracker. Some of the original pipe organ companies are still in existence, including Austin, Casavant and Schantz. Many new pipe organ companies are in business today such as C.B. Fisk, Buzzard, Lively-Fulcher, Ott and Ontko and Young. Certainly, many of these companies are involved in major projects in college and university chapels and auditoriums, symphony halls, cathedrals and churches. In addition to these companies, the major digital organ builders have increased prominence, including Allen and Rodgers. With Hammond organs entering the digital realm, they are now marketed by the Hammond-Suzuki company. Another category of business focus has developed that specializes in designing and replacing old pipe organ consoles, restoring pipe work, or adding digital voices to pipe organs. Such companies include Robert M. Turner Company, Eastern Organ Pipes, The McNeely Organ Company and the Walker Technical Company.

Before contacting organ companies, an organ committee should conduct as much research as possible about the companies they are considering. This book is designed to be an excellent reference source for doing this. They may be interested in securing the services of an organ consultant to help them in the search for an organ. Most importantly, they must have a good understanding of what the church's musical needs are in order to better ascertain what type of organ company might be best able to meet their needs. For example, a church with a growing contemporary music ministry would not need the services of one of the large pipe organ companies.

Many factors must be considered about the organ company that is being evaluated. Many of these same considerations apply when considering a piano or electronic keyboard for a church or other organization. The organ committee must ask and answer many important questions, which include but are not limited to the following:

1. Is the company independent or part of a conglomeration?
2. Does the company sell organs exclusively, or do they sell other instruments as well?
3. If the company sells electronic organs, do they have experience with pipe organs?
4. Is the company sales focused?
5. What kind of services does the company provide?
6. Is the company located in the immediate vicinity? (Pipe organ companies only operate from one site and do not have local representatives. Many digital organ companies have local representatives in most metropolitan areas.)
7. What is the level of corporate stability of the company? (Check Dunn and Bradstreet or similar report for review of financial stability.)
8. What manufacturing process is used to build their organs? custom instruments? "assembly line" approach?
9. What contract options are available? Does the company work with a standard contract or will they accommodate custom desires?
10. What is the potential for future growth of the company?
11. Has the company made any significant technological advancements?
12. How much money does the company spend on research and development of new technology? (Especially for digital pipe organ companies.)

As one can tell from the list, the organ committee must evaluate the business aspect of any organ company with which they may do business in addition to their musical effectiveness.

The following sections will acquaint the organ committee with most of the major pipe and digital organ builders in the United

States. Several other foreign organ companies are also mentioned. A brief description of each company is given, along with major characteristics of the company's products. Advantages and disadvantages of the company and their instruments are presented, as well as some of the notable installations of the company. This information is intended to give an objective review of the company and can be used in addition to literature obtained from the company themselves or from its website. As a type of "consumer's guide," this information will inform the committee without the bias of a representative of each individual company.

The Major Pipe Organ Companies in North America

Pipe organ companies in America are wide and varied in age and musical focus. Some companies have been in business since the late 1800's and several companies were founded in the mid 20th century. Some companies build only mechanical action (tracker) organs while others specialize in electro-pneumatic instruments. These companies also differ in the definition of the pipe organ itself. The membership of the Associated Pipe Organ Builders of America (APOBA) does not consider combination instruments to be true pipe organs. APOBA believes that the only suitable use of electronic voices in pipe organs is in 16' or 32' Pedal stops or orchestral voices.[1] There are several notable pipe organ companies that have embraced a more liberal use of digital pipe voices and are not members of APOBA to include the Austin Organ Company and Fratelli Ruffatti Organ Company.

Pipe organ companies are in great contrast with digital organ companies. There are also many differences between the various pipe organ companies. Most pipe organs are entirely custom instruments built to the musical desires of the customer and integrated with the architecture of the building in which they are installed. There are literally no two pipe organs that are exactly alike. Pipe organ companies use vastly different raw materials than digital organ companies. At a pipe organ company, one will most likely find wood and metal used to build the pipes rather than microprocessor boards that are found at digital companies. Digital companies may have libraries of recorded pipe voices, while many of the pipe companies make the pipes themselves. The pipe tuners in a pipe organ company are also trained to craft the actual pipes to make the desired sound rather than adjusting the digital parameters of the recorded pipe voices. Finally, pipe organ companies may only build one or two organs per year which may cost millions of dollars each. This is in contrast to digital organ companies which may install hundreds if not thousands of organs annually under a cost of $100,000.

A review of the major pipe organ companies in North America illustrates the diversity within the pipe organ industry itself. The full list of companies that are members of APOBA follows and websites for all companies are listed in Appendix E. A brief description of selected companies will be presented along with the major characteristics of the company.

Organ Companies that are Members of APOBA (not complete list)

Andover Organ Company
Buzard Organ Company
Casavant Freres
C. B. Fisk Organ Company
Dobson Organ Company
Goulding and Wood Organ Company
Holtkamp Organ Company
Kegg Pipe Organ Builders
Quimby Organ Company
Noack Organ Company
Ott Pipe Organ Company
Taylor and Boody Organ Company
Schantz Organ Company
Schoenstein and Company

Organ Companies that are not Members of APOBA

Austin Organ Company
Fratelli Ruffatti Organ Company

Reuter Organ Company
Rodgers Instruments, LLC
Wicks Organ Company

AUSTIN ORGANS, Inc.

The Austin Organ Company has been in business since the late 1800's. The company is particularly well known for their mechanical developments such as the universal air chest. In the early 1900's, they pioneered a new console type which was known for its reliability. The recent developments have seen an improvement in console cabinetry and the use of digital controls. Austin is one of the few pipe organ companies to embrace a more liberal use of digital voices than allowed by the APOBA. Several of their larger combination instruments have been built since 1995 in conjunction with the Allen Organ Company. Austin organs have been particularly favored by Presbyterian and Episcopalian churches across the country.[2]

Noted Installations
61 Stop Balboa Park Exposition Organ (1915), San Diego, CA
80 Rank Our Lady of Czestochowa Organ (1990), Doylestown, PA
Forbidden City Concert Hall Organ (1999), Beijing, PR China
108 Rank La Grave Presbyterian, Austin/Allen (1996), Grand Rapids, MI
162 Rank U. of Pennsylvania Organ (1926/2002), PA
138 Rank Fountain St. Austin/Allen Combin. (2003), Grand Rapids, MI
Harkness Chapel Connecticut College, New London, CT

Major Characteristics
-Universal Air Chest-electropneumatic controls
-Mechanical excellence and reliability
-Unique stop tab console design (traditional)
-Willingness to build large combination pipe/digital instruments

Advantages
-Experience in organ building
-Broad tonal philosophy, influenced by British organ builders J. W. Walker and Willis
-Use in computer aided design of pipe casework/integration with existing architecture

Disadvantages
-Uncertain corporate stability
-No longer a member of APOBA
-Liberal use of digital voices (for pipe purists)

CASAVANT FRERES

Casavant Freres was founded in Quebec, Canada, in 1879. Casavant is the major Canadian organ builder and one of the oldest in North America. The company has been largely influenced by the French school of tonal design. Casavant organs can be found in colleges, universities and conservatories throughout Canada and the U.S. in addition to cathedrals and churches. Although most of their instruments are two or three-manual instruments, many of their organs built in larger cathedrals and auditoriums are four and five-manual organs. Their website features many of their organs, to include the $4 million Rildia Bee O'Brien Clyburn organ at Broadway Baptist Church of Fort Worth, TX. This organ, Opus 3750, has 129 stops in 11 divisions comprised of over 10,000 pipes, and is probably the magnum opus of the firm.[3]

Noted Installations
Four-manual 82 stop Church of Notre-Dame, Montreal, Quebec
Latter Day Saints Temple Complex (Opus 3700), Independence, MO
Broadway Baptist Church (Opus 3750), Fort Worth, TX

Major Characteristics
-Experience in French school of organ building

-Return to mechanical action organs in the 1960's

Advantages
-French tonal focus
-Electric capture systems and combination action
-Since 1981, broad synthesis of classical, symphonic and modern tonal design

Disadvantages
-Not an American company-distance from headquarters
-Language barrier (possibly)

C.B. FISK, Inc.

The C. B. Fisk, Inc. was founded in 1961 by the late Charles Brenton Fisk in Glouchester, MA. As mentioned in the Organ History section, C.B. Fisk was a leader in the neo-baroque movement in the mid 20th century. Fisk was inspired by trips to Europe to study European instruments, and was especially influenced by Dutch organ builder Dirk Flentrop. Having formerly majored in nuclear physics, Fisk was highly educated and taught his employees by the Socratic method. Many Fisk pipe organs can be found in colleges, universities and concert halls across the U.S. These pipe organs are handcrafted mechanical action instruments that are specifically designed for the venue in which they are installed.[4]

Noted Installations
King's Chapel Organ (Opus 44), Boston, MA
Harvard University Memorial Organ (Opus 46), Cambridge, MA
Old West Church Organ (Opus 55), Boston, MA
House of Hope Presbyterian Church Organ (Opus 78), St. Paul, MN
Lay Mem. Organ Myserson Symphony Hall (Opus 100), Dallas, TX
Benaroya Symphony Hall Organ (Opus 114), Seattle, WA
Oberlin College Finney Chapel Organ (Opus 116), Oberlin, OH
Lausanne Cathedral Organ (Opus 120), Lausanne, Switzerland

Major Characteristics
-Mechanical (tracker) action
-Neo-baroque voicing, now embracing neo-Romantic also
-Technological innovation
-Opposition to integration of digital pipe voices
-Oak or pine hardwood used in wind chests

Advantages
-Member of APOBA
-Excellent reputation of building instruments for academic insti-
 tutions and concert halls
-Pipes made in Fisk factory
-Keyboards, drawknobs and all key desk components made in Fisk
 factory
-Organs assembled and played before shipping
-Excellent architectural concern-building modeled at scale with
 pipe casework

Disadvantages
-Cost-Fisk organs are on the upper end of the price spectrum
-Not well suited for the average church/average organist
-long lead time for instrument-at least 1 year in advance

LIVELY-FULCHER ORGAN COMPANY

The Lively-Fulcher Organ Company, which is based in Alexandria, VA, is owned by Mark Lively and Paul Fulcher. These men have experience with noted British organbuilder J.W. Walker and each has over 20 years of experience in the business. The firm's works are noted by an influence of 19th century organbuilder Cavaille-Coll. Many of the installations have electronic action, although the organ at the University of Utah Concert Hall is a mechanical action instrument. The noted installations below each have a stunning organ case, which is ornately constructed of finely carved wood such as cherry wood or African mahogany.[5]

Noted Installations
Christ Church Episcopal Cathedral, 60 Ranks, 2003, Nashville, TN
Cathedral of St. Matthew the Apostle, Washington, DC
University of Utah Concert Hall
St. Olaf Catholic Church, 67 Ranks, 2002, Minneapolis. MN
Christ Church, 51 Ranks, Exeter, NH (Planned for 2006)

Major Characteristics
-Experience in French school of organ building
-Three-manual instruments of roughly 50-60 ranks
-Well suited for liturgical settings and universities

Advantages
-French tonal focus
-Electric or mechanical action
-Customization in organ case to match architectural style of building
-Craftsmanship
-Skill in tonal voicing

Disadvantages
-Reasonably new company
-Smaller list of organ installations

FRATELLI RUFFATTI ORGAN COMPANY

The Fratelli Ruffatti Organ Company was founded in Padua, Italy, in 1940 by Antonio Ruffatti. The company has incorporated the traditions of excellence in European organ building as well as implementing technological improvements. Many local Rodgers Organ representatives are also representatives of Fratelli Ruffatti in the U.S. Ruffatti has great experience in building very large organs such as the Hazel Wright Organ of the Crystal Cathedral. This organ has the largest pipe organ drawknob console in the world with over 300 stop controls. Ruffatti organs are distinguished by their highly polished pipe facades and use of en chamade trumpet batteries.[6]

Noted American Installations
89 Rank St. Mary's Cathedral Organ, San Francisco, CA
62 Rank Baylor University Organ (1972), Waco, TX
147 Rank Davies Symphony Hall (1984), San Francisco, CA
117 Rank Coral Ridge Presbyterian Organ (1973), Ft. Lauderdale, FL
270 Rank Crystal Cathedral Organ (1982), Garden Grove, CA
79 Rank Spivey Hall Organ (1992), Morrow, GA
150 Rank Friendship Missionary Baptist Church (2005), Charlotte, NC

Major Characteristics
-Pitman wind chests-all electric normally used in American organs
-"Sipo" Mahogany imported from Africa used in pipe wind chests
-Pipes made in house
-Consoles made in house-first company to invent and develop solid
 state system
-Incorporation of digital voices
-Flexible tonal philosophy

Advantages
-All-electric wind chest vice pneumatic leather or slider wind chest
 for mechanical action (tracker)
-High quality pipe construction
-Organs assembled in shop before shipping
-Diversity of organ installations: churches, concert halls, academic
-Experience with very large organs
-Experience with combination organs
-Local representatives affiliated with Rodgers Organ representatives

Disadvantages
-Transatlantic shipping (cost included in instrument)
-Distance from the factory with local representatives in America
-Language barrier (possible)
-Not a member of APOBA

SCHANTZ ORGAN COMPANY

The Schantz Organ Company was founded in 1893 and is still

owned and operated by the Schantz family. The company has a general tonal approach to building organs and does not adhere to any particular school of organ voicing. Schantz has focused their business in building instruments for houses of worship and also has several noted installations for major academic settings or concert halls. Many of the Schantz organs are three-manual instruments of 30 to 60 ranks. Schantz focuses on pipe organs and does not build combination instruments. The Schantz website contains information about many recent Schantz organ installations.[7]

Noted Installations
118 Rank First Baptist Church Organ (1993), Orlando, FL
64 Rank Abyssinian Baptist Church Organ (1982), Harlem, NY
36 Rank First Presbyterian Church, Athens, GA
86 Rank St. Vincent Ferrer Catholic, New York, NY
Severance Hall Refurb (2000), Canton, OH
Melbourne Town Hall Organ Refurb (1999), Melbourne, Australia.
46 Rank Kirk of the Hills Presbyterian, St. Louis, MO

Major Characteristics
-Electro-pneumatic controls
-Broad tonal philosophy
-Freestanding organ cases when needed
-Architectural integration of organ case with sanctuary
-Has recently built an average of five organs per year

Advantages
-Experience in organ industry
-Focus on worship settings
-Member of APOBA

Disadvantages
-Not best suited for academic or concert hall venues
-Broad tonal approach

The Major Digital Organ Companies

In contrast to pipe organ companies, the digital companies will be described more on the basis of their technological features as related to the ability to represent the pipe organ. These companies rely more on technology than craftsmanship and vary in their relationship to pipe organs. Some companies focus on providing additions to the APOBA pipe organ builders. Other companies make combination instruments that have more than 50% digital voices. The remaining companies do not make combination instruments at all. Overall, these companies also vary in their efforts to replicate particular pipe organ builders or schools of organ voicing based on the organ samples that they use. Still other companies do not use a library of digitally recorded pipe sounds. These companies digitally replicate the tones produced by organ voices.

ALLEN ORGAN COMPANY

Much has been previously mentioned about the history of the Allen Organ Company. Allen led the digital revolution with the Allen Digital Computer (ADC) organ in the early 70's, and then developed the Master Design Series (MDS) organs in the 80's and 90's. The new Renaissance organs celebrate the heritage of the Allen company and add tremendous flexibility to digital organ design and voicing. Recently, the company has acquired the rights and drawings of the M.P. Moller Pipe Organ Company, which went out of business in the 1990's. This acquisition has advanced Allen Organs in the area of custom organ design. Allen is now much more capable of providing an upgraded custom organ console for an existing pipe organ.[8]

Allen has found a niche in the area of more traditional organ design. Allen organs are MIDI compatible and are now capable of being augmented with an expanded MIDI sequencer called the Allen Ensemble. The sound sequencer MDS Expander has a limited number of organ voices rather than the full set of GS MIDI voices. The company now is in a better position to market combination organs and has completed many important instruments. The tonal resources of an existing pipe organ can be expanded with the use of digital voices, especially 32' Pedal stops.

In 2004, Allen introduced several new technologies that add to their capabilities the Quantum Renaissance Organs were unveiled. They provide stop options of the American Classic, French Romantic, English Cathedral, and Baroque organs to be accessible in one organ through the Quad Suite technology. Additionally, the Acoustic Portrait feature allows the acoustic properties of virtually any setting to be selected for the Allen organ. This flexibility allows even more customization. The organist can select the desired registration as well as acoustic conditions for a given piece of organ literature to be played.[9]

Noted Installations:

Five-manual installations
Bellevue Baptist Church, Cordova, TN (365 stops, 241 ranks)
Prestonwood Baptist Church, Plano, TX (295 stops)

Figure 8 Five-Manual Allen Renaissance Organ.
(Bellevue Baptist Church, Cordova, TN)
Courtesy Allen Organ Company

Combination Instruments
108 ranks-Austin/Allen, La Grave Reformed Church, Lansing, MI
138 ranks-Schlicker/Allen, Peachtree Presbyterian Church, Atlanta, GA
179 ranks-Austin/Allen, Fountain Street Church, Grand Rapids, MI
38 ranks Collins/Allen, The Parish Church of Trono, Trono, Sweden

Digital Installations
Four-manual,221 stops, 157 ranks Tremont Temple Baptist Church, Boston, MA
Four-manual, 80 stops Cincinnati Symphony Hall, Cincinnati, OH
Four-manual, 70 stops Cathedral of St. John the Evangelist, Hong Kong
First United Methodist, Houston, TX (Three Renaissance organs -
-Four-manual, three-manual and two-manual in multiple locations
Three-manual Renaissance U.S. Coast Guard Academy Chapel, New London, CT

Major Characteristics
-Industry leader in customization
-E.M. Skinner American Classic sound for earlier Renaissance organs
-Largest distributor of digital organs in the world
-Now adaptable to real pipes
-Robust powerful sound (depending on the quality of the installation and voicing)
-20 bit sampling which is beyond CD quality
-Emphasis on symphonic string divisions on large organs
-English style reeds available

Advantages
-New Quad Suite allows four specifications in each Quantum Renaissance organ
-New Acoustic Portrait allows organist flexibility of choosing acoustics
-Extensive sample library which allows customized stop list
-Sturdy console construction

-Premium features standard-drawknob styles, coupler tabs, keyboard styles,etc.
-Custom design available on all organs
-Five-manual available
-Moving drawknobs standard
-Training resources for organists available on-line

Disadvantages
-Second voices can't be used individually
-Lighted drawknobs not available
-Very robust (loud)-this could also be an advantage if you really like to feel the pedal
-Not as experienced in combination organs
-Somewhat limited MIDI capabilities

CHURCH ORGAN SYSTEMS (formerly Baldwin Organs)

Baldwin organs have been produced since the 1950's. The company was originally based in Baldwin, Wisconsin, but has changed ownership and is now known as Church Organ Systems. The company is now also in partnership with Bevilacqua Pipe Organs. The company has not made its focus the electronic organs and is more focused in the piano market. However, the organ products are of high quality and produce a pleasant organ tone. The Church Organ Systems' marketing approach is rather interesting: instead of competing directly against the other companies, it openly provides information about their products. Links to competing digital organ companies can be found on the Church Organ Systems website. The website also has a several helpful resources for organists.

Major Characteristics
Experience in the music industry

Advantages
-Very economical prices which can be 40-50% less than other digital organ builders

-Great sound for the price
-Variety of sounds available
-Five-manual available
-Sturdy console construction
-MIDI compatible

Disadvantages
-Lighted drawknobs only
-Little experience in combination organs
-Questionable corporate stability

COPEMAN HART

This distinguished British company has been in business since 1960 and has a unique approach. Rather than using sample technology, Copeman Hart has tone modules that digitally produce the organ sounds. It has broad distribution within the British Isles, but are relatively unknown within the United States. Additionally, all of their products are fully customized and each instrument is built to the particular standards of each customer.

HAMMOND/SUZUKI ORGANS

In 1986, the Suzuki Company of Japan acquired the Hammond Organ Company. The marketing of Hammond Suzuki products in the United States officially started in 1989. The strength of the Suzuki company was its ability to resurrect the Hammond organ and introduce it to the digital age. Not only are traditional B-3 organs being built, but Hammond produces a line of commercial keyboards as well. They have crossed over into the traditional organ market by marketing the 900 series drawbar/classic combination organs. The new Concert Series organs now feature two and three-manual organs with traditional pipe sounds that have been digitally sampled. Hammond Suzuki also has improved the Leslie speaker, producing several updated versions that produce the traditional sound with updated technology. An important note is that Hammond Suzuki does not carry a parts inventory for Hammond organs built before 1985.

Noted Installations
926 Combo Organ, Second Calvary Baptist Church, Norfolk, VA
926 Combo Organ, Abyssinian Baptist Church, Norfolk, VA
926 Combo Organ, Rock Church, VA Beach, VA
Vintage B-3*, Union Memorial United Methodist, St. Louis, MO
Vintage B-3*, Metropolitan Baptist Church, Washington, DC
Vintage B-3*, Bethel Institutional Baptist Church, Jacksonville, FL

*-These churches also have pipe or digital organs.

Major Characteristics
-New digital tone wheel sound generation
-Great for contemporary/gospel music churches
-Often used in jazz or blues music
-Uses drawbars instead of drawknobs or stop tabs
-Sound based on the flute sound of the organ

Advantages
-Tone wheel sound
-Flexibility of combination traditional/tone wheel organs
-Incorporation of MIDI as well
-Sturdy console construction
-Standardization allows people to be able to play the Hammond
  organ with minimal training

Disadvantages
-Concert Series does not have a competitive pipe sound with indus-
  try leaders
-Vintage B-3 models are not available
-Not the preferred instrument for classical or traditional music
-Non-AGO pedal boards
-The basic Hammond does not contain principal, string or solo
  voices

JOHANNUS ORGANS

Johannus Organs built in the Netherlands is among a rich tradition of European organ builders. Although relatively unknown in the United States, Johannus Organs is probably the second largest electronic organ company in the world (by units sold), after Allen Organs. They recently constructed a new factory in the Netherlands. Of note, the company once featured the highest sample rate of any digital organ company, using 20 bit samples. The company now uses 24 bit samples. Several other companies now meet or exceed this sampling. They offer a wide range of organs, from two-manual practice instruments to large customized organs. Their challenge in the US is to compete against Allen and Rodgers, who own the market share in this country.

Major Characteristics
-Tradition of Dutch organ making

Advantages
-24 bit sampling-once highest in digital organ world
-Long samples
-1 Digital to Analog converter per stop
-4 Mb of information per stop

Disadvantages
-Lack of exposure in U.S.
-Combination instruments not available

RODGERS INSTRUMENTS, LLC

The Rodgers Instruments, LLC, is one of the youngest of the digital organ companies, but has the greatest experience in combination organs, having built over 3300 organs with pipe work. Additionally, it is the only digital organ company who has built complete wind-blown pipe organs without digital voices. In 2001, Rodgers Instruments formed a new relationship with the Pinchi (pronounced '*pinky*') Pipe Organ company, also of Italy. Of recent years, Rodgers has led the way with technological advancements that are features of real pipe organs. Rather than focus on individual pipe samples, they have focused on the ensemble sound in PDI technology. They are the only company to offer stereophonic bi-amplified sound. The company has previously restricted its customization of products to mainly four and five-manual instruments. As of 2005, two and three-manual instruments can be obtained with a great degree of customization as well. Most three-manual instruments contain a rather generous standard stop list that is augmented by a battery of second voices that can be individually selected. The company has upgraded console craftsmanship in recent years. Lighted and moving drawknobs are now optional as part of the new customization packages.[10]

The most recent update is that Rodgers Instruments unveiled the Rodgers Organ Architect in February of 2005 that brings unprecedented customization to their organs. Previously, only four-manual organs provided the flexibility of customization for Rodgers. Three-manual organs and smaller were fairly standard models with a generous stop list for flexibility. However, customization of these instruments was limited to moving drawknobs, wood lattice music rack, and console stain. The Rodgers Organ Architect is a web-based program that allows the customer to select specification, drawknobs, keyboard style, couplers, music rack, organ bench, and other features once limited to four-manual organs. These new organs will be referred to as the Trillium Masterpiece series, which introduces 11 new organ types.[11]

Noted Installations:

Pipe Organs:
Five-manual Second Baptist Church, Houston, TX (Rodgers)

Combination Organs:
150 rank E.M. Skinner/Rodgers, Christ Episcopal Church, Needham, MA

151 rank Casavant/Rodgers, Bel Air Presbyterian Church, Los Angeles, CA
100 rank Schleuter/Rodgers, Ebeneezer Baptist Church, Atlanta, GA
Three-manual 960, Bethel Institutional Baptist, Jacksonville, FL
-has four ranks of pipes
Three-manual 960, Webster Hills United Methodist, Webster Groves, MO
-has 21 ranks of Moller pipes

Digital Organs:
Three-manual 960, First Cathedral, Hartford, CT
Three-manual 960, First Congregational Church, New London, CT
Three-manual 945, Green Trails United Methodist, Chesterfield, MO
Two-manual 835, Union Memorial United Methodist, St. Louis, MO

Major Characteristics
-Aeolian-Skinner sound-Later American Classic
-Tremendous technological advancements-Parallel Digital Imaging
-Excellent flexibility for MIDI
-24 bit sampling which exceeds CD quality
-Very fiery chorus reeds

Advantages
-Part of the multimillion dollar Roland Group-excellent corporate stability
-Introduction of Rodgers Organ Architect in 2005 allowing unprecedented customization for Rodgers organs
-Rich, clear ensemble sound with two digital samples per note
-Only company to have bi-amplified stereophonic sound
-Pipe organ features: dynamic wind, random de-tuning, Swell expression
-Leadership in MIDI
-Diverse stop list with Rodgers Sound Library optional
-Independent additional voices, voice palette
-More experience in combination organs
-More contemporary flexibility

Disadvantages

-Custom features once only available in four manual-previous emphasis on 'stock models'

-Older two and three-manual organs are 'stock models'

-Not many five-manual installations

-Lighted drawknobs once standard through three-manual (moving drawknobs are now available in Trillium two, three and four-manual organs)

-Moving drawknobs previously at added cost equal to comparable specifications with most organs

Walker Technical

Walker Technical has been a leader in digital sound production for over 30 years. Founded in the hills of Pennsylvania by Bob Walker, the company spends little effort on publicity, but is one of the most respected and well-known companies in the field. Walker Technical has been involved with pipe organ companies in particular and provides digital extensions to pipe organs. Some of the most well-known pipe organs in the country are augmented with Walker digital pipe voices, including the Crystal Cathedral Hazel Wright Organ, the First Congregational Church Organ of Los Angeles, the U.S. Naval Academy Chapel Organ. Their additions to pipe organs include 32' Pedal stops, foundations and Solo stops, and blend perfectly with the real pipe voices. Walker Technical also specializes in the field of custom digital theater organs. Their main competition in this market is the Allen Organ Company. They have not, however, focused on the market of classical digital pipe organs.

While Rodgers and Allen market primarily digital organs that are compatible with pipes, Walker is operating on the other end of the spectrum. Walker specializes in providing digital voices to pipe organs and supplies these voices to many pipe organ companies. As such, Walker is in a league of their own and have created a niche market in which there is minimal competition. Having completed 1500 to 2000 projects over the past decade, Walker technical is one of the leading companies who has conducted combination organ projects.

Walker Technical is a leader in the field of digital organ sound reproduction. Their marketing strategy is the polar opposite of the major digital organ companies in the U.S.; they rely on word of mouth and have minimal formal advertising. They provide a tremendous service for churches that have pipe organs and are limited by size or budget as to how the organ can be expanded. In many cases, adding a few Walker digital voices can have a tremendous effect on the tonal quality and versatility of a pipe organ. As low key as their approach is, you may have already heard Walker digital voices as part of a larger pipe organ without even knowing it.[12]

CHAPTER 7:

Organ Builders and Companies

*T*his chapter will provide the organ committee a glimpse at several different pipe and digital organ companies. These descriptions are based on my personal experience of having visited each company and having a chance to speak with their representatives. Visits were made to the Allen Organ Company, world headquarters, the Austin Organ Company C.B. Fisk, Inc., and several local Allen and Rodgers organ representative showrooms. A review of these companies will illustrate the manufacturing process of several organ types (digital and pipe), and a few different business models and marketing approaches for distribution. This information will give the organ committee an idea of what to expect when interfacing with the organ companies they choose to contact.

1. Acker Church Organ Company, Virginia Beach, VA

Founded in 2002 by John Acker, the Acker Church Organ Company (ACOC) is a representative of Rodgers organs. Mr. Acker has over 26 years of experience in the church organ industry and has been involved with both pipe and electronic church organ firms. ACOC has taken a unique marketing approach by offering products direct to the consumer rather than wholesale. By eliminating the overhead costs of operating a large showroom, he is able to pass on significant savings to churches in search of an organ.

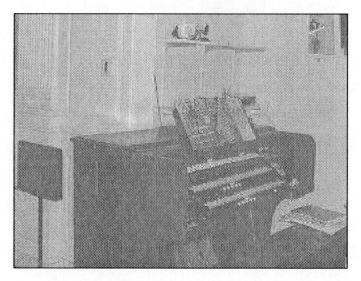

Figure 9 Old Wicks Console in Organ Pit
(Galilee Episcopal Church, Virginia Beach, VA)

The focus of the company is allowing a church to decide what musical option is best for it: a completely digital instrument, added digital voices to a pipe organ or a new organ console with added digital voices. ACOC is also teamed with R. A. Daffer Church Organs (to be discussed later), which allows more flexibility in the pipe options available. A perfect example of this teamwork is the organ project at Galilee Episcopal Church on the Virginia Beach oceanfront. The church had an older Wicks pipe organ of roughly 20 ranks that was not meeting the needs of the congregation. The console was severely worn and the tonal resources of the organ were limited. With the help of the ACOC, the church decided to pursue a combination pipe/digital organ with a Rodgers Trillium 967 console. The combined instrument has over 100 ranks and is one of the largest combination organs in the Hampton Roads area. R.A. Daffer was supporting the project by providing assistance in rewiring the electro-pneumatic pipe controls, which would be controlled from the new Rodgers console. [1]

Figure 10 New Rodgers 960 Console in the Organ Pit
(Galilee Episcopal Church, Virginia Beach, VA)

2. Allen Organ Company, Macungie, PA

While en route to Groton, CT, in 2001, I had a chance to visit the Allen Organ Company Headquarters with my wife and daughter while returning from vacation. We arrived in Macungie shortly before 5 pm, and were able to catch Scott Clark just before closing. I had studied organ with Mr. Clark in Syracuse, NY, while I was working on my master's degree at Syracuse University. As you enter the facility, your eyes are drawn to a three-manual organ with pipework in a rotunda, in which several two-manual organs were located. With the administrative offices off to the left, the famed Octave Hall is to the right of this grand entrance. Octave Hall is used for the many concerts that are sponsored by Allen Organs on some of their best instruments by noted artists such as Carlo Curley and Diane Bish. The huge stage in Octave Hall is quite amazing; using a rotating platform, up to three organs can be featured at a time. A four-manual Renaissance console and a four-manual Allen theatre organ were featured. Mr. Clark played a stirring arrangement of "Praise the Lord, Ye Heavens Adore Him" on the four-manual Renaissance organ, complete with reverse-colored keyboards, maple drawbars and wooden coupler tabs. We were quite impressed by the power of the organ and its tonal qualities in this impromptu demonstration.

Figure 11 Five-Manual Allen/Moller Console
(LaGrave Reformed Church, Lansing, MI)
Courtesy Allen Organ Company

Beyond Octave Hall is an enormous display area that is a testimony to the impressive history of the company. On display are the first Allen organ, Allen's transistorized organ, the first digital organ, and several other items of Allen memorabilia. Also on display is a 'sculpture in pipe', that once adorned the Moller Pipe Organ Company. Being able to see these organs, amplifiers and speakers from years of Allen development brought to life Mr. Markowitz's book <u>Trials and Triumphs of an Organbuilder</u>. Unfortunately, we were not able to see the actual manufacturing portion of the factory, which is located in a separate facility from the actual headquarters building. Hopefully, we'll be able to attend a concert at Octave Hall and walk through the Allen history display in the near future.

3. Austin Organ Company, Hartford, CT

Our tour of the Austin Organ company took place in December of 2001, while many of the factory employees were enjoying a holiday vacation. The tour included major areas of their design and construction facility. On display in their design room were many pictures of Austin organs. Several architectural drafts of organ designs in various churches were also featured. In this area, the designers produce renderings of the pipe work and casing that would best complement the architectural style of the room in which the organ will be installed. Some degree of computer graphics technology is used in their design process.

We then viewed the area where the electro-pneumatic controls are being built. As a key is depressed, it produces an electrical signal that leads to a pneumatic device made largely of leather. The electric signal produces a magnetic charge that causes a leather pouch to contract or expand. As this happens, a valve opens or closes, porting pressurized air from the chest into the applicable pipe. One of these pneumatic devices is made to operate each pipe in an organ.

Next on the tour was the area in which the pipe voicing takes place. Pipe voicing is divided into the type of pipe that is involved, to include flue (principal and flute) as well as reed pipes. Each type of pipe is voiced by its own voicer, a craftsman experienced in finishing their particular class of pipe. Reed voicing is most complicated because of the different mode of sound generation than flue pipes. Reed pipes make sound as a resonator magnifies the sound made as air passes over the shallot. A tuning wire controls how much the shallot is allowed to vibrate.

Pipes of a particular rank are placed on a rack similar to the pipe chest that they will eventually rest on. An air chest is also available to produce wind that will be used to play the pipes. A short keyboard that can move the length of the pipe chest is used to play the pipes. The voicer makes adjustments to each pipe as required to ensure they are in proper tune and producing the desired sound. The final voicing is conducted on site once the pipes have been installed in their final location.

In the Pedal pipe shop and shipping area, the larger pedal pipes are constructed. This large warehouse contains sets of pulleys that can be used to hoist the huge 32' pipes in place. This area also contains the foundry where the metal pipes are poured from molten metal. The wooden pipes are machined in this area as well. Another area of the factory is dedicated to console construction. Two very elaborate consoles were in various stages of construction. One was a five-manual console slated for the University of Pennsylvania and the other a three-manual console. The craftsmanship on the consoles was very impressive. The stop names were color coded to match the representative family and the stop jambs divided the stops for each division with ornate decoration. Interestingly, the weight of the consoles themselves has been drastically reduced due to the use of digital technology. Microprocessors are used to take the input from the keyboards and stops selected to produce the appropriate electrical signal that operates the pipe control system.

Representatives of the Austin Company were generous enough to provide a wide selection of Austin Organs discography, to include recordings of Thomas Murray and Carlo Curley. Of note, many of the recent organs featured in the recordings contained substantial amounts of digital voices. One organ was built in conjunction with the Allen Organ Company of Macungie, PA.

4. C. B. Fisk, Inc.

The C. B. Fisk, Inc. is located in Glouchester, MA, about 30 miles northeast of Boston. We first toured the facility in January 2004 guided by Mark Nelson, a senior designer. The tour started in the Fisk design room, where 1:16 scale models of Fisk installations are on display. These models include the Myerson Symphony Hall and the Seattle Symphony Hall organs. The organ designers begin the design process with the model of the sanctuary or auditorium. They then insert models of the organ case. Once the model design is selected, it is inputted into a computer aided design (CAD) program. The CAD program allows the designers to achieve a greater degree of definition in the design and to make changes as necessary.

C.B. Fisk builds one pipe organ at a time. Fisk organs are mechanical action instruments and are at the high end of the pipe organ spectrum in terms of cost. We saw the scale model for the organ then under construction which is now installed in Christ Episcopal Church of Roanoke, VA, (Opus 124). This instrument was be completed in the spring of 2004. Prior to shipping, the organ was assembled as completely as possible and played to enable craftsmen to correct any major mechanical or voicing problems. The company holds an open house each time an organ is assembled to allow organ enthusiasts (and potential customers) to hear their latest opus. Currently, there is a five-year backlog of instruments under contract for the firm. This backlog has ranged from 3 to 8 years due to the varying demand for Fisk pipe organs.

One of the largest areas in the facility is the wood working shop. In this area, consoles, mechanical action assemblies, wind chests and Swell boxes are constructed. Mr. Nelson demonstrated the use of roller assemblies which translate the movement of a pedal or manual key being pressed down to the mechanical linkage. As this happens, the slider located on the wind chest shifts, allowing air to be available for all of the pipes sounding that particular note. On top of the wind chest are pipes for all 61 notes of each rank of pipes in a particular division. The mechanical controls from the stop drawbars align all of the pipes in a rank to be playable. This overlapping mechanical matrix allows the pipe to sound which corresponds to the note(s) played and stop(s) selected. A Swell box was also under construction in which the Swell shades had been installed. The operation of the Swell shade is also mechanically controlled by the Swell Pedal on the organ console.

We next went into one of the storage rooms where the two keyboards for the Christ Episcopal Church organ and boxes of pipes that were ready for the next installation were contained. The keyboards were very useful in understanding how the key sticks are constructed. A wooded key stick is the foundation for each of the 61 keys of the manual keyboard. Each key stick is approximately 18" long. The 3" or 5" of the key that is actually visible (natural or sharp keys) is covered by ivory or ebony material for most keyboards. This particular keyboard was reverse-colored; having dark brown grenadilla naturals and off-white rosewood sharps with bone caps. Mr. Nelson then explained the parts of a flue (toe, foot, mouth, ears, languid and body) pipe and reed pipe (shallot, body, resonator) using several of the pipes in storage. The company constructs all pipes in house and begins the manufacture about six months before the organ is completed.

Finally, we went to one of the large assembly areas which stored several Bourdon pipes. These pipes are excellent examples of pipes constructed of wood that are stopped at the top end, producing tones an octave lower than their length suggests. This area also contains a very new voicing table, on which a rank of pipes can be tuned to produce the desired pitch and sound quality. This is one of the two areas in the factory that is large enough to assemble a complete organ for final voicing and adjusting prior to shipping. In this area, metal pellets of lead, tin, and/or copper are melted and poured in troughs to make sheets of composite metal. These sheets are rolled to form the organ pipes.

In March of 2004, we attended the Open House at C.B. Fisk for Opus 124, the Christ Episcopal Church organ of 38 ranks. Having seen the 1:16 scale model several months prior, the actual organ was quite impressive. Hundreds of people from the community joined a select group from the church to experience the first breaths of this great organ. The church organist put the organ through its paces, although final voicing will take place later in the church. This was the culmination of seven years of patient waiting for the completion of the instrument. The church had previously housed a pipe organ that became unplayable due to mechanical and structural problems with the organ case. During the years without an organ, the church used a Yamaha Clavanova keyboard for leading the worship.

The organ is a two-manual instrument with pedal clavier. No expense was spared and no detail was forgotten in the crafting of this beautiful instrument. The console is built into the organ case and is made of cherry. The stop knobs are made of french polished walnut and have hand lettered labels. The case stands roughly 25 feet tall and is constructed of a rich Honduran mahogany. The case contains all of the organ's pipes, blower and mechanical linkages.

The facade pipes are made of polished hammered spotted metal and are all speaking pipes. Doors on either side of the case allow access to the inner workings of the organ and allow one to understand the arrangement of the mechanical key action.[2]

The rich tonal quality of the organ was audibly apparent, although the organ was assembled in one of the shipping areas. The organ is comprised of 26 individual voices between a Great, Swell and Pedal. Six of the eight Pedal stops are shared with the Great. The stops selected are of French character. This organ is a perfect example of quality over quantity. Every aspect of the instrument is first class and meets the intent of its design. The purpose of this instrument is clear from its parameters: to render organ literature specifically of the French school, to lead the choir in anthems, and to lead the congregation in the liturgy.

C.B. Fisk, Inc. is an important element of the pipe organ world. The company definitely upholds the tradition of fine pipe organ building. There are no attempts by Fisk organs to unnecessarily overwhelm by huge stop lists or contemporary features. Their organs are simply handcrafted works of art that are mechanically robust and will be in service for many decades to come.

5. Jordan Kitts Temple of Music (Allen Organ Company)

The Allen Organ Company representative in Virginia Beach, VA, is located within Jordan Kitts Temple of Music. The showroom includes several models of Allen organs within an enclosed room separate from the rest of the pianos that are sold by Jordan Kitts. The advantage of this type of arrangement is that lower prices may be available due to the higher volume of the piano/organ business. The disadvantage may be that there is less specialization on the part of the dealership with respect to organs. Additionally, such a business arrangement has an overhead cost of operating a large facility and filling it with pianos and organs that must eventually be sold. The Allen Organ representative here services the southern Virginia area and may also service North Carolina.

6. Marshall Ogletree Associates

In November of 2002, I attended an open house at Marshall Ogletree Associates in Needham, MA. Marshall Ogletree is the Rodgers Organs representative for the New England area. The open house featured the Trillium and Insignia instrument lines and demonstrated the great flexibility of Rodgers instruments. In the demonstration hall five of the Trillium instruments were positioned, each voiced to simulate a different acoustic environment or school of organ building.

The organs were voiced as follows:

Organ	Voicing
Trillium 967	E. M. Skinner organ
Trillium 957	Aeolian Skinner organ
Trillium 927	New England chapel organ
Trillium 837	Theatre organ
Insignia 577	Baroque organ in reverberrant cathedral

Members of the Marshall Ogletree staff played pieces that were representative of music that would have been composed with the particular organ in mind. For example, the "E.M. Skinner" organ was used to play the "Tuba Tune" by Lang, featuring the 8' Tuba stop on the organ. The 8' Tuba is an alternate stop to the 8' Festival Trumpet. These and other changes were part of the voicing process for each organ.

Following the open house, a concert was given by Felix Hell on the four-manual Rodgers combination organ at Christ Episcopal Church of Needham, MA. The organ incorporates the 1940's Aeolian-Skinner organ originally designed as a theatre organ for the Yankee Radio network in Boston. The organ was sold in the late 1950's to Christ Episcopal Church and moved into the sanctuary. In the 1970's, the organ was revoiced to the American Classic style by removing theatre and orchestral voices, adding new principal and mixture stops and lowering the wind pressure of the instrument.

Rodgers Organs signed a contract in 1996 to build a four-manual

custom console and computerized control system for the pipe organ. Additional digital voices were also added. Marshall Ogletree was involved in the design of the console, built by Rodgers, and conducted the final organ voicing. The McNeely Organ Company of Waterford, CT, rewired the pipe organ. The final combined instrument boasts of 110 digital ranks and 51 pipe ranks, making it the largest combination instrument in the world at its inception. [3]
This organ demonstrates many valuable lessons:

1. Organ pipes themselves are virtually timeless investments.
2. A pipe organ can be altered for different functions (theatre organ/church organ).
3. A used pipe organ can be an excellent purchase.
4. For a pipe organ, the console and pneumatic action are the limiting components, not the pipes themselves.
5. Digital voices can be used very effectively to augment any pipe organ.
6. Buying a completely new pipe organ is rarely an absolute necessity.

Both the Allen and Rodgers Organ companies have built numerous fine combination organs. Rodgers was first to fully embrace the combination organ concept. Jerome Markowitz, founder of Allen Organs, was a staunch proponent of the completely electronic instrument. After his passing, his son Steve Markowitz, has guided the company to actively compete in the market for combination instruments. In fact, they have teamed with Austin Organs to build many fine combination instruments.

7. R.A. Daffer Organs

R.A. Daffer Organs is the largest distributor of Rodgers Organ by volume worldwide. Daffer Organs also represents Fratelli Ruffatti pipe organs of Padua, Italy. Their showroom is located in Jessup, MD, in the outskirts of Baltimore. I had an opportunity to visit Al Murell of R.A. Daffer at the showroom in the spring of 2002. On display was a diverse array of Rodgers organ consoles. The first was a stunning four-manual Rodgers custom console awaiting installation in an area church. The console had moving drawknobs and couplers. Other consoles included a new Trillium 957 and an older three-manual Rodgers analog organ. These two organs were connected to speakers that were strategically placed in the showroom.

My first introduction to a major R.A. Daffer installation was the Hampton Minister's Conference and Organist and Choir Guild Workshop at Hampton University in June of 2000. R.A Daffer organs provides a large three-manual organ for the worship services in the Hampton University Convocation Center which seats over 4,000. That year, a Rodgers 950 was provided for the Convocation Center. With quite an impressive battery of speakers behind the several hundred voice choir, the organ was more than adequate to have a commanding presence in the large venue. This is contrary to the idea that you need a four or five-manual organ for such a large space. The smallest three-manual, the Rodgers 927, was located on the stage of the hall and used for the Master Class, taught by Dr. Carl G. Harris of Hampton University. R.A. Daffer also has a display booth in the Convocation Center that provides information on all of the Rodgers organs as well as the Roland VK-77 Praise Combo. Each year, Don Lewis, is on site to demonstrate the VK-77 to the public.

8. Rodgers Organs of St. Louis, MO

Rodgers Organs of St. Louis is also part of a business that represents Steinway and Baldwin pianos as well. Ken Kohler is the local Rodgers representative there. The showroom is a cross between Jordan Kitts Temple of Music and Marshall Ogletree. The organ showroom is almost as large as the Marshall Ogletree showroom. The center of the showroom is a three-manual Rodgers 967 in front of several ranks of pipes. Four additional Rodgers organs were also on display, in addition to a custom two-manual Walker digital organ that had been built in an older Rodgers organ console. My experience with Ken Kohler of Rodgers Organs dates back to 1992, when my home church selected Rodgers to install their new two-manual 835 organ.

I was able to visit Rodgers of St. Louis most recently in October of 2003. During this visit I was able to play both the Rodgers 967 and the Walker two-manual custom organs which will be reviewed later. (Rodgers was planning another large three-manual installation in the St. Louis area which involved a Rodgers 967 being interfaced with several ranks of pipes and custom Walker digital samples.) The Rodgers 967 I played was used several weeks later by the St. Louis Symphony orchestra in an organ concerto. In addition to using the organs in the showroom for demonstration purposes, Mr. Kohler frequently takes organ committee members to churches that have Rodgers organs installed. In our first visit to the old showroom in 1992, I was struck by his low-key approach. He allowed us to be impressed by the sound of the Rodgers organs we heard played without bombarding us with data about the organs features.

CHAPTER 8

Instrument Reviews

$\mathcal{T}$he information in this chapter is intended to give a glimpse at the instruments that can be found in a wide spectrum of churches and worship centers. Pipe organs will be presented followed by digital organs. In general, the order is largest to smallest. Specifics of the organ installation are included which includes the company that built the instrument, the size of the instrument and major characteristics of the instrument. If multiple instruments (pianos, keyboards, or Hammond organs) are used, this will be noted. Stop lists of the individual instruments are not included in the descriptions. More specific information about the instruments can be obtained from the church directly or, in many cases, from their websites. This chapter will illustrate the wide spectrum of instruments that can be found in a variety of worship settings across the United States.

PIPE ORGANS

1. 210 Rank M.P. Moller/Goulding and Wood Four-Manual Pipe Organs - Basilica of the National Shrine of the Immaculate Conception (Washington, D.C.)

The organs at the National Shrine were both originally built by the M.P. Moller Organ Company. The main instrument is located in the gallery of the Basilica, and is the larger of the two instruments at 152 ranks. The chancel organ, which serves as an antiphonal organ, is located in the front chancel area and is comprised of 58 ranks. Improvements to the organs were made in 2000 and 2001 by the Goulding and Wood Organ Company. A new four-manual console was built for the gallery, which allows control of all 210 ranks of the organ. This new console features many new technological improvements. Sequencing capabilities allow the organist to record and play back their own playing for analysis. Stop combinations can be saved on a floppy disk for the use of multiple organists. Additionally, a new three-manual console was built for the chancel organ. Goulding and Wood also supervised the relocation of the balcony organs Positiv divisions. Additionally, new pipe ranks were added in the expansion.

The stop lists for the combined instrument can be found on the Goulding and Wood Company website. A careful review of the list is quite instructive. The Gallery organ is comprised of the following divisions: Great, Swell, Choir, Positiv Left, Positiv Right, Bombarde and Pedal. The Great division contains a full Principal chorus, four mutation stops and two mixture stops. The division also contains three Violone stops, speaking at 32', 16' and 8'. The Swell division is very generous and is marked by three mixture stops. The Positiv divisions are comprised of principals, flutes, mutations, mixtures and each has a single reed stop. The Pedal division is very profound; it contains a 64' Gravissiment resultant stop, five stops at 32' and a wide variety of stops of representative organ stop families. Lastly, the Bombarde division is marked by a 16' Bombarde Harmonique, 8' Trumpette Harmonique and 8' Pontifical Trumpet. The Chancel organ is comprised of Great, Swell, Choir and Pedal divisions. In comparison to the Gallery organ, the Chancel organ is considerably smaller. However, its 58 ranks make it in reality larger than pipe organs of many churches across the country.

The organs are featured at the Basilica's Summer Recital Series, featuring organists from across the world. The July 10, 2005 concert was played by organist Dr. Mickey Thomas Terry. The programme selected by Dr. Terry demonstrated the flexibility of the organs. The program selected included works of Dupre, Mark Fax, Robert A. Harris, Bach and Vierne. These pieces were used by Dr. Terry to demonstrate the full dynamic range of the instrument, from the quieter flutes and celestes to the triumphant roar of full organ. The excellent acoustics of the National Shrine resulted in a reverberation of at least five seconds following the completion of several of the more robust pieces.

2. 103 Rank M.P. Moller Four-manual Pipe Organ - U.S. Naval Academy Chapel (Annapolis, MD)

The 103 rank pipe organ at the Cathedral of the Navy was built by M.P. Moller Company of Hagerstown, MD, one of the largest organ companies in the United States. The organ was installed in the 1940's and has been expanded several times. Controlled by a four-manual console on a moveable dolly, the organ is contained in several main divisions. The console is quite ornate and is adorned by wood carvings that match the theme of the pulpit, lectern and altar in the chancel area. To the right and left of the chancel area, the Great, Swell and Pedal divisions are contained. Unenclosed pipe chests for the Positiv divisions are located on both sides of the chancel above the choir stands. The Antiphonal division is located in the back of the chapel above the balcony and includes a Trumpet en Chamade division. The Antiphonal organ is also controlled by a two-manual console located in the balcony.

The organ was preserved in 1991 while the chapel was renovated and air conditioning was installed. During that period, a Rodgers 945 three-manual digital instrument was used to lead the chapel services. The organ is under the care of the Robert Pierce Pipe Organ Service which has also performed several additions in the late 1990's. The organ is a vital part of the excellent music program of the Naval Academy which is directed by Dr. John Talley. As part of the chapel music program, the organ is featured during the annual presentations of the Messiah and during as frequent organ concerts. Since the early 1970's, the organ was presided over by the late Mr. James Dale, an organist of great renown within the U.S. and abroad. Following his untimely death in 1995, Mr. Monte Maxwell has served as the chapel organist, continuing the great tradition of excellent organ music at the Naval Academy.[1]

Figure 12 M.P. Moller Organ
(U.S. Naval Academy Chapel, Annapolis, MD)

The Moller organ will be further expanded in 2006 using digital voices from Walker Technical. This expansion is being made possible by a very generous gift to the USNA Music Department by one of the USNA alumni classes. Over the past decade, the organ has been expanded by the addition of new pipe and digital voices. However, space limitations in the Chapel precludes the additional of new pipe ranks. The only available option for expansion of the organ is to add digital voices. In addition to the added voices, Walker Technical will build a new five-manual organ console to control the expanded instrument. The organ's existing four-manual console will be relocated to the Chapel balcony, replacing the more limited two-manual console. The expanded instrument is expected to be the largest five-manual combination instrument in North America.[2]

3. Aeolian-Skinner Pipe Organ - Trinity Church-Copley Square (Boston, MA)

The three-manual Aeolian Skinner organ at Trinity Church is a great instrument of 124 stops and 133 ranks. The original nave organ was built by E.M. Skinner in 1926, followed by the

Aeolian-Skinner Chancel organ in 1963. The organ is comprised of nine divisions. The nave and chancel organs each having Great, Swell, Choir and Pedal organs and a nave solo division. Amazingly, the resources of all nine divisions are controlled from the three-manual console. This is an interesting example of a very large organ (over 100 ranks of pipes) controlled by a three-manual console. Having so few manuals may limit the organist's flexibility in use of the vast resources compared to a console of four or five manuals. Indeed, some organs with more versatile consoles may have half as many stops. Three of the five 32' Pedal stops of the nave Pedal division are electronic. The nave solo division contains many orchestral stops characteristic of E.M. Skinner.

4. 64 Rank Schantz Five-manual Pipe Organ - Abyssinian Baptist Church (Harlem, NY)

We had an opportunity to hear this fantastic organ while worshipping at Abyssinian Baptist Church in December 2002. The organ was installed in 1978, and is one of the largest organs in the United States. Under the current leadership of Dr. Calvin Butts, Abyssinian was formed in 1808 by Ethiopian immigrants, and has been in Christian service for almost 200 years. Once pastored by the late Drs. Adam Clayton Powell, Sr. and Jr., the church has been a bulwark of the African American community. In addition to their strong Christian and civil leadership, Abyssinian has a great music program, under the direction of Minister of Music Dr. Jewel T. Thompson.

The 64-rank pipe organ has a powerful presence in the worship service. The instrument spoke majestically from the great hymns of faith, to the stirring anthems of the choir and carols of the Advent season during the communion period. The five-manual organ console is located in the raised choir loft behind the pulpit area. Pipe divisions are located in chambers in the left and right front corners of the sanctuary. Exposed pipe ranks are located behind the choir in the center of the loft. An Antiphonal division speaks from the rear of the church. This organ was a tremendous investment of the church and is now likely worth several million dollars. As the great congregation moves forward, it will do so with the power and authority of a great organ as they give praise to God in worship. Further information about the church and the organ can be found at the church's website: www.abyssinian.org. The organ's stop list can be found at www.nycago.org/Organs/html/AbysBapt.htm. The organ does not have many mutation stops other than the Swell division. By having a five-manual console, the organist has more flexibility in playing this instrument.

5. Three-manual M. P. Moller Pipe Organ-Metropolitan Baptist Church -(Washington, D.C.)

The M.P. Moller pipe organ was installed in 1985 when Metropolitan, under the leadership of pastor Dr. H. Beecher Hicks, Jr., moved into a new edifice. The organ speaks from pipe chambers directly behind the chancel area with several ranks of pipes exposed. The Trumpet en Chamade extends horizontally from the organ case and has a commanding presence. The three-manual console is located in the chancel area and faces the choir so that the organist's back is to the congregation. The organ is used along with the grand piano and Hammond organ during worship. The organ pipes are mostly hidden behind a cloth screen accept for a few ranks of principal and flute pipes and the Trumpet en Chamade which extend out from the organ case above the choir loft. This instrument has a great deal of character and displays tonal qualities of many other Moller organs. The only drawback is that the rather contemporary, carpeted sanctuary makes the reverberation almost nonexistent. The church is making plans to move to a larger edifice in 2006 and has selected a new instrument for the edifice under construction in Largo, MD.

I had a chance to play the instrument in September of 2004, after having relocated to the Washington, D.C. area. I was reminded of several facts that are characteristic of many organs:

1. The organ sounds much different in an empty sanctuary than when it is filled with worshippers on Sunday morning.
2. The organ sounds much different at the console than further back in the sanctuary. The different organ stops are much clearer and almost more 'Baroque' sounding from the console.

3. The organ sounds different in different locations in the sanctuary. The organ is not quite as loud in the balcony as on the main floor. Also, the organ's sound does not reach the seating area in the back of the sanctuary. This section is directly under the balcony which reduces the sound from the open seating area in the front of the sanctuary.

Metropolitan's Moller has approximately 40 stops throughout the three-manual instrument. The manuals are named Great, Swell and Positiv. Although the Positiv is under expression, it does not contain any string stops. The Great contains an 8' Trumpet which is quite strong and the majestic Trumpet en Chamade speaks from the Positiv division. The Swell has the usual complement of stops from the principal, flute, string and reed families, although the only reed stop speaks at 8'. The Pedal division is probably my favorite, and contains the standard principal and flute 8' and 16' stops. The reed voices of the Pedal include a pungent 16' Fagott and a commanding 32' Contre Bombarde.

Figure 13 Three-Manual Moller Pipe Organ
(Metropolitan Baptist Church, Washington, D.C.)

6. Austin Three-manual Pipe Organ - Shepherd of the Seas Chapel (Groton, CT)

This large organ was donated to the Navy in 1982 and relocated to the chapel by the McNeely Organ Company of Waterford, CT. The organ pipes and console are located in the balcony of the large building with an Antiphonal division in the chancel area. The organ was built in the 1950's by the Austin Organ Company of Hartford, CT. The tonal quality is much like many of Austin's organs with very broad principals and flutes. Interestingly, the mutation stops are all found in the Great division and there are none in the Swell. This installation shows the advantages and disadvantages of pipe organs rather clearly. The organ is a great investment and provides a solid foundation for the music department. However, the organ also requires maintenance and tuning, which is not always done as often as needed. The organ console itself is one of Austin's standard three-manual "battleship" designs with stoptab controls. This instrument would be a great candidate for an updated digital organ console with additional digital ranks (especially in the Swell). Unfortunately, the inability to commit to regular maintenance prevents the organ from being in a condition to be featured as a recital instrument, although it is probably one of the largest instruments in this area of Connecticut. The instrument demonstrates the utility of a used pipe instrument.

Figure 14 Austin Pipe Organ Case
(Shepherd of the Seas Chapel, Groton, CT)

7. Two-manual 23 stop C.B. Fisk, Inc. Tracker Pipe Organ - St.
   John's Episcopal Church (Niantic, CT)

I was introduced to this fine organ in August of 2004 by Dr.
John Anthony, who is organist at the parish. The organ is the second
mechanical action (tracker) organ that I have played, both built by
the C.B. Fisk, Inc. of Glouchester, MA. This instrument was
installed in 1988 after the church had identified the need for a new
organ in 1981. The many years in between were devoted to the
organ committee search process, fundraising, and the design,
construction and installation of the instrument. This organ is
located in the rear balcony of the church. The 400-seat sanctuary is
in a modified A-frame construction, with a trapezoidal cross-
section. The height of the room allows plenty of space for the freestanding organ case which complements the modern architecture of
the building. The case is constructed of quarter-sawn white oak, and
stands approximately 20 feet tall. As with other tracker organs, the
console is part of the organ case and is located on the front side
under the organ facade.

The organ was designed by the late Charles B. Fisk, then president and founder of the company that bears his name. Although a modest 23 stop instrument, this organ has more tonal color and variation than many three-manual instruments of over 40 stops. The organ is effectively a three-manual instrument organized in two-manuals. The lower manual is the Great organ, which also shares fundamental principal stops with the Pedal. The 16' Prestant of the Great and Pedal are the facade pipes in the front of the organ case. Behind those pipes are the remaining pipes of Great and Pedal divisions. The Great is built upon the principal chorus, several ranks of flute stops, a five-rank Mixture, three-rank Sesquialtera and an 8' Trommeten (trumpet). The Pedal adds a16' Posaune which is located on the base of the balcony at the rear of the organ case. The upper manual plays both the Swell and the BrustPositiv. The Swell was designed after the French organs built by Cavaille-Coll. This division is marked by a beautiful four-rank Cornet, Hautbois and flute Harmonique. The BrustPositiv is modeled after a German Brustwerk division and is located behind moveable doors above the console. This division has several ranks of flutes, a Zimbel and 8' Regal (German reed). Both Swell and BrustPositiv are controlled by ventils which allow either or both division to be playable on the upper manual.

Figure 15 C.B. Fisk, Inc., Opus 93 Organ Case
(St. John's Episcopal Church, Niantic, CT)

Dr. Anthony demonstrated the capabilities of the organ by playing several pieces. Using a basic hymn, he demonstrated the Great and Pedal divisions. The Great can also be coupled to the Pedal by way of a foot lever. The 8' Octava has a full fundamental tone, which is enhanced by the 4' Octava. The 2' Superoctav can be drawn to add more of the upper work and its drawknob can be double drawn (pulled out fully) to add the Mixtur V. The 8' Spillpfeife and 4' Rohrflote are both very distinct flute stops. The Sesquialtera III can be double drawn with the Rohrflote. The Great reed is a 8' Trommeten which is a German stop of full tone.

The Swell demonstration illustrated the versatility of this division with only six stops. The 8' Chimney flute and 4' Spitzflute form the foundation of the division. The 8' flute Harmonique is double drawn from the Chimney flute drawknob and the Cornet IV is double drawn from the Spitzflute. The 8' Hautbois and Trompette add to the battery of stops that can be used as solo voices or as part of the full Swell. The Swell box is located in the rear of the organ case above the Pedal Posaune pipes. The Swell shades are operated by the only expression pedal on the organ and has the feel of mechanical operation. The BrustPositiv is a small division that can be used for German Baroque music or for a type of continuo. With the doors fully closed in front of the BrustPositiv pipes, the volume and timbre of the stops are changed considerably.

Figure 16 C.B. Fisk, Inc., Opus 93 Key desk
(St. John's Episcopal Church, Niantic, CT)

After Dr. Anthony's demonstration, I was able to play several pieces on the instrument. One piece was the Allegro Maestoso from Mendelssohn's Organ Sonata II. I played this with only the Great 8' Octava and 4' Octave, and the Pedal 16' Prestant 8' Octava and 8' Trommeten. The character and tonal beauty of these few stops was sufficient to make a very commanding registration for this jubilant piece. A fuller registration may have been overwhelming, as later demonstrated by Dr. Anthony. These few stops did not need the upper work of 2' and Mixtur to add more brilliance. I've played the same piece on a new digital instrument, on which I selected a much fuller registration and even had the Swell coupled to the Great.

Here are a few lessons learned from this encounter with this fine Fisk tracker instrument:

1. A large number of stops is not necessary if the available stops have character of sound.
2. A solo division is not absolutely necessary and three divisions can easily be combined in a two-manual instrument.
3. A mechanical action (tracker) requires minimal maintenance.

This organ requires reeds to be tuned about once a year. There is no leather to wear out and be replaced and no electronics to go "squirly" at most inopportune times.

4. With a custom designed organ, the organ case can be designed to complement the architectural theme of the building.

5. A freestanding organ case does not take up that much room. This instrument has a 'foot print' of about 10'x8', which is not too much larger than a large four-manual organ console. The pipes and mechanical linkages have been arranged within the case to maximize the use of space. The blower, for example, is located on the top of the case above the Swell box.

6. Even a small congregation is able to purchase a fine pipe organ. The main requirement is constancy of purpose, dedication to the effort, and focus.

7. For a pipe organ, the priority is the pipes. Nonessentials such as a third manual, couplers, or combination action can be sacrificed to support the number of pipes needed.

This modest pipe organ of only 23 stops has had a profound impact on my outlook on organs (pipe and digital). The lessons learned above convey much about the tracker organ. Much has been said about the C.B. Fisk organ company and their great artistic work. This instrument is a fine example of their creativity, genius, craftsmanship and dedication to musical excellence. An organ does not have to be massive to be impressive. If the instrument is expertly crafted for the room in which it speaks, its magnificence is in the relationship to that space tonally and visually, and its ability to fulfill the purpose of its primary use.

DIGITAL/ELECTRONIC ORGANS

1. Allen Custom Four-manual MDS (1985) - De Witt Community Church (Syracuse, NY)

I was able to play this organ while taking organ lessons with Scott Clark, who is now an area manager for the Allen Organ company. The organ is featured on the cover of Jerome Markowitz's book <u>Trials and Triumphs of an Organ Builder</u> and is one of Allen's finest organ installations. Built with a four-manual console, the organ has a very broad stop list. With the organ speaker chambers on both sides of the chancel, the organ was also graced with a strong Antiphonal division. This organ is pre-Allen Renaissance technology and has a tremendous pipe-like sound. As I recall, the organ was characterized with lush strings, a stately Tuba stop in the Antiphonal, and a very robust Pedal division complete with 32' Untersatz.

The large four-manual console is located in the chancel area behind the altar. This location provides an excellent position for the organist to hear the organ's sound in the sanctuary. The speakers are located in chambers to the right and left of the chancel area. The antiphonal division speaks from the balcony's corresponding speakers. The organ's sound is so powerful that you can feel the vibration at the organ bench when playing with a full registration.

2. Rodgers 960D

a. First Congregational Church (New London, CT)

I was able to play this instrument as installed in First Congregational Church in New London, CT. The church purchased the instrument to replace an aging pipe organ and had decided to install the digital voices alone and leave the pipe work. The 960D is a three-manual console with 67 main stops. With second voices, the organ is comprised of over 100 ranks of digital voices combined. The organ console is located in the choir loft in the back of the church. With the facade pipes of the old pipe organ that was replaced still in tact, most worshippers are unaware that the organ is a digital instrument.

The voices on the 960 are quite good when selected individually and when used in ensembles. Of particular note is the 32' Pedal Contre Bombarde, which is particularly powerful. Second voices on the voice palette add to the stops that are visible on each drawknob. Each drawknob with a dot above the stop name has at least one additional stop available through the voice palette. This is a standard feature on all Rodgers Trillium and latest PDI organs. These voices are independently controlled by the digital display under the Great/Choir drawknobs. To access this feature, "set" is pressed as the drawknob is pulled. This displays the stop name on the digital display. By rotating the selector wheel counterclockwise, the additional voice(s) can be accessed.

b. Bethel Institutional Baptist Church (Jacksonville, FL)

I have heard this organ during worship at Bethel several times during 2002 and 2003. Bethel is a historic African American church co-pastored by Drs. Rudolph McKissick Sr. and Jr. The Minister of Music is Mr. Omar Dickenson, who heads a very diverse music ministry. The church's choirs render traditional hymns and anthems as well as contemporary and traditional gospel.

The organ is a unique installation in a 3000 seat sanctuary that is asymmetrical. The organ console is located to the right of the pulpit area in a platform for the instruments. The choir loft extends to the right and is topped by organ chests with two ranks of pipes. To augment the music ministry, the church also uses an 8' Steinway grand piano and a vintage Hammond organ and several MIDI keyboards in addition to the Rodgers. The music ministry of Bethel is an excellent example of the diversity of music within an African American church and the multiple instruments that are part of achieving excellence in music ministry.

3. Allen Renaissance 330 Three Manual (1999)

I was able to play this organ previously installed in the Allen Organ showroom in Jordan Kitts Temple of Music in Virginia Beach, VA. It was installed with full speaker complement, which at full organ could virtually blow you out of the showroom. The 330 was one of Allen's newest instruments which featured the then newly released Renaissance technology. Some of the stops on the 330, especially the flutes, are almost better than real pipes. Most impressive is the Harmonic flute in the great manual. The swell has very nice String stops, and the choir is dominated by Erzahler stops of 4', 8' and 16' pitches and celestes. The Pedal has a 32' Contre Bombarde and Contre Violone. Although most of the

Reeds are English styled, there is a Festival Trumpet in the Choir. Unfortunately, the second voices in each division must be used together and cannot be controlled independently. The console package featured the 50th anniversary edition with wooden keyboards and drawknobs with maple stems. This organ would be great for a medium to very large church.

4. Rodgers 835 Two Manual (1992) - Union Memorial United Methodist Church (St. Louis, MO)

This organ is located in my home church. A committee chosen to oversee the selection process heard a similar organ at Green Trails United Methodist Church and that visit included someone who was ready to provide the financial means to make the purchase possible. That person was renowned opera diva Grace Bumbry who made the donation in memory of her mother, Mrs. Melzia Bumbry and in honor of her father, Mr. Benjamin Bumbry. Both had been long time members of Union Memorial and Ms. Bumbry spent her early years singing at church. Her dedication to the project and my strong encouragement led to the installation during the summer of 1992 under the pastorate of now Bishop Rhymes Moncure.

The church had suffered for many years with a decreasingly reliable Baldwin from the 1950's, I suggested that the church purchase a new organ. The Baldwin was operated by vacuum tubes that were housed in a closet in the Sacristy. This closet contained the acolytes robes and was really steaming by the end of a long communion service, due to the heat produced by the tubes.

Figure 17 Rodgers 835 Console
(Union Memorial United Methodist Church, St. Louis, MO)

The organ is one of Rodgers first generation PDI (Parallel Digital Imaging) organs and has a tremendous pipe sound. It was installed by Ken Kohler and his son Franz of Rodgers Organs of St. Louis. The two-manual instrument has about 40 stops and is a very comprehensive instrument. The speakers for the Great organ are mounted on both sides of the chancel and the Swell speakers are in the back of the chancel behind the choir. The Antiphonal organ is located in the back of the nave above the balcony. The only draw-back of the installation is that the location of the console in the choir loft is actually behind the Great speakers. This makes hearing the organ somewhat difficult from the organist's bench unless the Swell is coupled to the Great.

I was fortunate enough to be in town for the installation of the organ during summer leave and was able to assist in the installation of several of the speaker cabinets. In July of 2002, I conducted an organ workshop/demonstration at the church featuring the Rodgers 835 and the new Hammond B-3 which is a recent addition to the music ministry. Under the leadership of Dr. Lynn Mims and Minister of Music Mr. E. Don Morris, the church made a transition to a more contemporary worship style. The Rodgers is used in the early traditional service, while the Hammond is the mainstay for the contemporary 11:00 service.

5. Baldwin Custom Two-manual (1995)/Hammond 926- Second Calvary Baptist Church (Norfolk, VA)

When Second Calvary built a new edifice in the early 1990's, Baldwin Organs was contracted to build a digital organ for the church. Second Calvary is pastored by Dr. Geoffrey V. Guns. Dr. Ernest Brown, then Minister of Music at Second Calvary and Professor of Music at Norfolk State University, chose the specification for the organ. The instrument is a two-manual console that was positioned in the choir area, giving the organist the ability to hear the organ which is contained in speaker chambers to the left and right of the choir loft. The stop list is similar to the Rodgers 835 or Allen 230, but has additional stops. The Pedal division's 32' Untersatz speaks from speakers behind the choir, and provides a great bass presence to the instrument. Several MIDI voices are also available to the organist on either the Swell or Great. Although the Baldwin Company, which now makes organs as Church Organ Systems, is more widely known as a fine piano maker, their opus at Second Calvary is a fine instrument.

Second Calvary's diverse music ministry is supported by a 8' Baldwin Grand Piano, which was purchased in 2002. The instrument has a very rich robust sound and provides accompaniment for the church's choirs. Additionally, a Kurzweil keyboard is used for many of the contemporary Gospel songs. With a vibrant music ministry, Second Calvary's instruments are used to worship God in many musical genres. This is not uncommon to many African American churches in the Hampton Roads Area that seek to embrace contemporary music in the midst of celebrating a rich musical heritage.

In 2004, the church removed the Baldwin organ and replaced it with a Hammond 926 organ, providing more contemporary flexibility. The new organ provides several advantages. The church music ministry has transitioned to a more contemporary format. The new organ supports this change in focus and provides the renowned

Hammond tone wheel sound. The traditional Hammond sounds are controlled by drawbars similar to the B-3 organ. In addition to the tone wheel sounds, the organ has the added flexibility of traditional pipe organ voices which are accessible by tilt tablets. Additional specifics of this instrument will be presented in the next section. Overall, the Hammond organ is a great option for churches that have a strong Gospel or contemporary music focus, but who still want some traditional pipe organ sounds for hymns.

6. and 7. Hammond 926 (2002) and Hammond CS-235 (2002)

I was able to play both of these new instruments by Hammond Suzuki Incorporated in November of 2002 at the Piano and Organ Warehouse of Virginia Beach, VA. The 926 is Hammond's combination instrument that combines the drawbars with traditional organ stops. A two-manual instrument with 32 note concave Pedal board, the 926 has nine drawbars for the Great and Swell, an 8' and 16' for the Pedal and has representative pipe organ stops for each manual and Pedal as well. The drawbars and stops can be used by themselves or together and the selection is independent for each manual. There is also a battery of MIDI voices that are accessible on each manual. Both the drawbar and traditional sounds are digitally sampled and Hammond has developed an updated Leslie speaker that comes with the organ. Although the instrument was located in a small room, I was not overly impressed with the quality of the pipe samples. This organ is a great instrument for a church that emphasizes contemporary or gospel music, but wants to have the flexibility of a traditional pipe sound. The pipe sounds, however, may not satisfy a church that is accustomed to a real pipe organ or recent digital instrument.

The CS-285 is one of Hammond's Concert Series models, built as a traditional pipe organ. This instrument is a three-manual organ with self contained and external speakers. The pipe sounds are digitally sampled and can be adjusted by the organist. Several tone controls can be chosen to vary the character of the organ sound. This provides the ability of the organ to sound like a traditional pipe organ, have a southern gospel sound or a theatre organ sound.

Again, the organ was housed in a small room, so I was unable to determine how the instrument would sound in a larger sanctuary. Overall, the instrument would be an inexpensive option for a church that wanted a good deal of flexibility.

CHAPTER 9

Postlude

*T*his book has presented information about the modern organ in the 21st century. As foundational information, a review of the major organ companies of the early 20th century provided a springboard for study of the modern pipe organ. The developments of electronics brought about the creation of the first electronic organs in the early 1930's. A foundation for understanding technologies used to build electronic instruments was gained by investigating the Hammond organ and early electronic pipe organs. Basic knowledge of the organ also served to provide basic information about organs for members of organ committees or other readers of this book.

In the year 2005, we are in a great period of the evolution of the organ. Many pipe organs built in the early 1900's are still in service after possibly several refurbishments and upgrades. The advances of digital technology since the 1970's has brought about a revolution in the electronic organ which has made them much more like the pipe instruments they seek to replicate. The maturing of the combination pipe/electronic organ has also come to fruition. Most digital organ companies and many pipe organ companies are incorporating a hybrid approach to their new organ projects. By the inclusion of MIDI in the palette of organ capabilities, the traditional organ has been transformed into a virtual control station to blend traditional and contemporary voices seamlessly.

The traditional pipe organ world has come to respect the contributions of the digital organ companies and the instruments they produce. As the organ world becomes even more flexible and open to changes, the future is very promising for the organ. In many cases, there is 50 to 100 years of data to illustrate the long term cost of purchasing and maintaining a pipe organ. In contrast, since the development of the electronic organ, it is clear that their life span is roughly 20 to 30 years. Enough information is available to assist any church at reasonably estimating the cost of a pipe or digital instrument. With fiscal concerns in mind, the prudent organ committee should form an independent assessment of their options with the best of stewardship in mind.

The future of the organ is very exciting. Expect to see the following in the next 20 years of organ development:

1. Most new organs built will be hybrid pipe/digital instruments.
2. Digital organs will be more customized.
3. There will be a resurgence of the organ in contemporary worship.
4. Increased sample rates of digital voices will make them much more pipe-like.
5. Much larger organs will be possible to the average church with the use of digital voices.
6. Aging pipe organs will be upgraded with state of the art digital consoles and digital voices.
7. Only the best pipe and digital organ companies will survive and will build combination instruments to some extent.
8. Organists must adapt to the changes in musical tastes and adapt more contemporary music in their repertoire.

My hope is that this book will be useful to members of organ committees who are in search of new instruments for their worship centers and sanctuaries. Additionally, this book should be a welcome addition to the libraries of pastors and musicians who serve in churches throughout the country. The information presented will be a springboard for further study of the organ, pianos, keyboards and MIDI. The intent is that more people would have access to information that will help increase knowledge of these instruments. Rather than seeing the use of instruments based on a popular fad, we can hope to achieve some balance in our worship so that all instruments are appreciated for their ability to worship and praise Almighty God.

Appendix A

Organ Committee Guide

IDENTIFY THE NEED

What are the primary uses of the organ?

_____Lead congregational hymns

_____Traditional

_____Gospel

_____Accompany anthems

_____Play formal organ literature

_____Baroque

_____Romantic

_____Contemporary

_____Organ concerts/recitals

_____Academic instruction/organ lessons

_____Contemporary music for praise and worship

_____Traditional gospel songs

_____Contemporary gospel songs

What is the budget available for the organ?

_____< $10,000

_____$10,000-$25,000

_____$25,000-$50,000

_____$50,000-$100,000

_____$100,000-$200,000

_____$200,000-$500,000

_____$500,000-$1,000,000

_____Over $1,000,000

How large is the worship center/sanctuary?
_____Seats 100-500

_____Seats 500-1000

_____Seats 1000-2000

_____Seats 2000-5000

_____Seats over 5000

What is the level of training or proficiency the organist(s) that will play the organ have?

_____doctorate in organ performance

_____masters degree in organ performance

_____masters degree in music (piano or choral)

_____undergraduate degree in music

_____advanced musical training

_____average musical training

_____no formal training; does not read music

How large is the choir or choirs the organ will accompany?

_____10 to 30 voices

_____30 to 50 voices

_____50 to 100 voices

_____100 to 200 voices

_____over 200 voices

What features are required in an organ?

_____Two-manuals-Great/Swell and Pedal

_____Three-manuals-Great/Swell/Choir and Pedal

_____Four-manuals-Great/Swell/Choir/solo and Pedal

_____Five-manuals-Great/Swell/Choir/solo/Positiv and Pedal

_____Pipes

    _____Electro-pneumatic controls

    _____Mechanical (tracker) controls

_____Pipes and digital voices

    _____Using pipes from existing pipe organ

    _____Using new pipes

_____Digital voices

_____Hammond B-3 sound

_____Custom stop specification (stop list)

    _____Baroque organ voices

    _____Romantic organ voices

    _____American classic organ voices

_____MIDI (musical instrument digital interface) capable

What optional features are desired?

_____Moving drawknobs

_____Wooden keyboards

_____Custom console finish

_____Custom finish drawknobs

_____Acoustic enhancement system

_____Moveable console

_____Back rest

_____Wood lattice/solid wood music rack

_____Sound sequencer

_____Hammond B-3 and classical organ voices

Appendix B

Registration Guide

Information presented here provides additional details about registration. An excellent resource for information about organ stops and registration is <u>The Organists Manual</u>, by Roger E. Davis. Another good resource on organ stops is the website www.organstops.org. This database has a comprehensive list of virtually every organ stop imaginable as well as a description of the stop and several organs that contain the stop.

Mutation Stops

A stop marked 2 2/3' sounds one octave plus a perfect fifth (or 12 diatonic notes) above the unison pitch of the key played. A 1 3/5' stop sounds two octaves plus a pure third (17 notes) above the unison pitch of the key played. A 1 1/3' stop sounds an octave higher than the 2 2/3' stop. Compound mutation stops can also be found in the Pedal. A 32' Resultant stop can be made by combining a 16' stop and a 10 2/3" stop. A 64' Resultant can be similarly made using a 32' stop and a 22 1/3' stop. The flute mutation stops include the Nazard 2 2/3' and the Tierce 1 3/5', while the principal mutation stops include the Twelfth 2 2/3' and the Tierce 1 3/5'.

The following lists common stop names for the major classifications of organ stops based on the country of origin. Stops are listed from lower pitched stops (16') up to higher pitched stops (4' or 2'). Pedal stops begin with stops commonly found at 32'. The accepted color coding scheme is also used on drawknobs and tilt tabs of many organs: foundations (black), flutes (blue), strings (green), reeds (red).

This guide can aid the organist in understanding the stops that are available on many different organs. For the pianist who plays the organ, this guide will be especially useful. By identifying the predominant country of origin of stops on an organ, the school of organ building can be determined. For example, if an organ has principal stops "Diapason" and "Erzhaler" flute stops, the organ is probably built in the English/American style. If the organ's principal stops are "Montre," "principal " or "Prestant" and flute stops "Bourdon doux" and "flute Harmonique," it probably follows the French school of organ building.

Common Stop Names:

Foundation
French: Montre, Principal, Prestant, Doublette
German: Prestant, Prinzipal
English: Double diapason, Diapason, Super Octave

Flute
French: Bourdon doux, Bourdon, Flute Harmonique
German: Gedackt, Hohlflote, Rohrflote, Blockflote, Koppelflote, Spitzflote, Waldflote
American: Harmonic flute, Erzahler, Klein erzahler

Strings
French: Gamba, Viole de Gamba, Gamba Celeste, Viole Celeste, Unda Maris
English: Salicional

Reeds
French: Bombarde, Hautbois, Trompette, Cromorne, Cor Anglais, Clairon, Chalumeau
German: Waldhorn, Rankett, Krummhorn, Nachthorn, Schalmei
English: Double Tromba, Tromba, Tuba Regal, Tuba Magna, Trumpet, Clarion

Pedal

French: Contre Bourdon, Contre Bombarde, Contre Basson, Montre, Principal, Prestant, Basson, Subbass, Quinte, Clairon, Doublette
German: Untersatz, Contre Posaune, Fagott, Gedeckt, Posaune, Quinte, Nachthorn, Rohrschalmei
English: Contre Ophicleide, Resultant, Tuba Profunda, Diapason, Ophicleide, Tuba, Choral Bass, Super Octave
American: Contra Violone, Violone

Mutation

5 1/3'-Quinte
2 2/3'-Nazard (French), Nasat (German), Twelfth (English)
1 3/5'-Tierce (French), Terz (German)
1 1/3'-Larigot (French), Nineteenth (English)
1'-Scharf (German), Twenty-second (English)

Mixture

French: Plein Jeu, Cymbale
German: Zimbel
English: Mixture, Cymbal

Solo (all 8' voices)

French: Hautbois, Trompette en Chamade, Cor Anglais, Voix Humaine
German: Menschenstime
English: Oboe, Tuba Mirabilis, Royal Trumpet, English Horn, Vox Humana

Appendix C

Pricing Comparison of Major Electronic Instruments
(Estimates in 2005 dollars)

Organ	New	Used
Allen/Rodgers Custom four-manual	$110,000+	
Allen 80 Stop/Rodgers 967	$100,000	$85,000
Allen 58 Stop/Rodgers 957	$85,000	$65,000
Allen 50 Stop/Rodgers 927	$65,000	$50,000
Baldwin/Johannus large three-manual	$60,000	
Allen MDS-75	N/A	$35,000
Allen 44 Stop/Rodgers 837	$50,000	$35,000
Hammond 926	$40,000	$28,000
Hammond CS-230	$40,000	$28,000
Hammond B-3 (digital)	$30,000	
Rodgers Newport 830	N/A	$12,000
Rodgers 840	N/A	$ 9,000
Allen MDS-60		
Rodgers 330 (analog)	N/A	$ 8,000
Rodgers 220 (analog)	N/A	$ 5,000
Rodgers 110 (analog)	N/A	$ 3,000
Allen MDC-20	N/A	$ 2,000

Appendix D

Useful Resources

1. Reference Material
American Guild of Organists: www.agohq.org
American Institute of Organ Builders: www.pipeorgan.org
Musicom: www.musicom.com
N Time Music: www.ntimemusic.com
Organ Historical Society: www.ohs.org
Organ Specifications: www.theatreorgans.com
Wheat Works Productions: www.wheatworkspro.com

2. Pipe Organ Companies
A.E. Schlueter Pipe Organ Co.: www.pipe-organ.com
Austin Organ Company: www.austinorgans.com
Casavant Freres: www.casavant.org
Eastern Organ Pipes, Inc.: www.eopipes.com
Fisk Organ Company: www.cbfisk.com
Full Organ Console Design: www.fullorgan.com
Holtkamp Organ Company: www.holtkamporgan.com
Lively-Fulcher Organ Company
Noack Organ Company: www.noackorgan.com
Ontko Pipe Organ Company: www.ontkopipeorgans.com
Martin Ott Organ Company: www.martinottpipeorgan.com
Schantz Organ Company: www.schantz.com
Taylor and Booty Organ Company
Wicks Organ Company: www.wicks.com
Henry Willis and Sons, Ltd: www.willia-organs.com.

3. Digital Organ and Keyboard Companies
Allen Organ Company: www.allenorgans.com
Allen Organ Studios: www.allenorganstudios.com
Church Organ Systems: www.churchorgansystems.com
Chapel Music Company: www.chapel-music.com
Copeman Hart Organs: www.copeman-hart.com
Hammond Suzuki Organs: www.hammondus.com
Johannus Organs: www.johannus.com
Jordan Kitts Temple of Music: www.templeofmusic.com
Kurzweil Keyboards: www.kurzweil.com
Marshall Ogletree Associates: www.organpower.com
R. A. Daffer Organs: www.dafferorgans.com
Robert Tall Associates: www.tallassociates.com
Roland Instrument Corporation: www.roland.com
Rodgers Instruments LLC: www.rodgersinstruments.com
Steinway Piano Company: www.steinway.com
Technics Keyboards: www.technics.com
Yamaha Keyboards: www.yamaha.com

4. Used Organ Resources
Allen Organs Wholesale: www.allenorganswholesale.com
B3 World: www.b3world.com
Ebay: www.ebay.com
Keyboard Exchange: www.keyboardexchange.com
Keyboard Trader: www.keyboardtrader.com
Organ Clearing House: www.organclearinghouse.com

Glossary

Analog sound - a direct signal derived from a sound source that reflects the frequency of sound waves. A continuous representation of a sound wave rather than the discrete levels of digital representations. The human ear can only hear an analog sound representation. Digital sound must be converted to an analog signal to be heard.

Analog Electronic Organ - Early electronic organs built from the 1930's. These organs used analog tone generators or oscillators to make the organ tones for each stop. Tone generators were used to simulate the sound of the organ stops of a particular organ. Most electronic organ builders discontinued use of analog tone generation systems by the late 1970's.

Antiphonal division - A division of the organ that produces sound from the pipes or speakers that are located at the opposing end of a sanctuary (or auditorium) from the main instrument.

Budget - A detailed analysis of costs associated with an expenditure of funds; it usually explains expenses planned over the scheduled work period for purchasing or maintaining the organ. The budget for a pipe organ has more long term implications than the budget for an electronic organ due to the longer manufacturing process of the pipe organ. Design and construction of a pipe organ may take several years while most electronic organs can be installed within a period of months.

Choir division - A division of the organ that is played from the bottom manual of a three-manual organ; it contains flue and reed stops. In addition, in contrast to the Positiv (Positive) organ, it also contains string stops and is under expression.

Combination organ - An organ comprised of pipes and electronically generated pipe stops. The sound comes from speakers that are usually hidden within the pipe chambers, in addition to the pipes themselves.

Convolution - mathematical computations used by the Allen Organ Company to recreate the reverberation properties of selected venues (i.e. famous organs in cathedrals or auditoriums).

Couplers - Mechanisms which allow different manual keyboards (manuals) to be played together in different ways. They also allow pipes normally played by the keyboards to be played on the pedal keyboard. They are often engaged by rocker keys located above the keyboards, but may appear in various locations on pistons, drawknobs, toe studs, etc.

Digital - A representation of an analog signal which corresponds to an amplitude of sound for a given time period. (The shorter the time period the greater the definition of the digital representation.) This results in a better representation of the analog source. Digital signals must be converted back to analog using a digital to analog converter (DAC) in order to be played through the speakers and heard by the human ear.

Digital to Analog Converter (DAC) — A microprocessor that converts digital signal into an analog signal in digital organs. Some digital organ builders use one DAC for each organ stop. Other organ builders combine the notes to be played using software and then convert the combined digital signal into an analog signal which is sent to the speakers.

Diapason - A foundational stop of the pipe organ. It is the name for an 8' principal stop on an English organ.

Digital Electronic Organ - Electronic organs that use digital samples of real pipe organ voices as the source for organ tones. In the early 1970's, the Allen Organ Company used technology being developed by the Rockwell company that was also used in calculators and personal computers to develop the first digital electronic organ. Current technology allows many digital organ builders to provide pipe samples from various real pipe organs. These companies have a library of digital samples, allowing for organs with customized stop lists to be built.

Digital Voice Module - A digital circuit board containing DSP (Digital Signal Processors), a reverberation system, DACs and sample memory.

Drawbars - Controls on the Hammond organ that adjust the intensity of each fundamental tone. The tones represent a basic flute tone at 16' pitch through 1', including fractional pitches. The presets on the left side of the Hammond are reverse-colored keyboards that activate preselected combinations of drawbars.

Drawknobs - Controls on the pipe organ console that select a stop to be played or coupler. The name of the stop or coupler is engraved on the face of its drawknob. Mechanical drawknobs are pulled out to select the stop and are pushed in to deselect the stop. Lighted drawknobs light when pulled out to indicate the stop selected and spring back into place once released. The light goes out when the drawknob is pressed in.

Expression - The ability to control the volume of a division of the organ. This is accomplished by adjusting the position of the corresponding expression pedal located on the bottom of the console above the pedal board. The organist controls the expression pedals with the feet. For pipe organs, the Swell, Choir and Solo divisions are under expression. In some digital organs, all divisions are under expression.

Fidelity - The similarity between the original live sound wave and its analog or digital representation.

Flash memory - A type of non-volatile computer memory that stores information in the organ such as piston preset combinations. This type of memory acts as RAM, but is actually a solid state device. This device functions only using electronics and does not depend on an external source of power to maintain the memory. Another example of flash memory is the phone numbers stored in a contact list on a cell phone.

Flue pipe - A basic organ pipe made of metal or wood in which the tone is created by the movement of the column of air in the pipe. Ranks of flue pipes are designated principal, string or flute stops. Flue pipes are in contrast to reed pipes.

Great division - The main division of the pipe organ; it is played from the bottom manual of a two-manual organ or the middle manual of a three-manual organ. This division contains the most robust stops of the organ and is not usually under expression. The Great organ or "Grand Jeu" on a French organ is always located on the bottom manual.

Interpolation - A process which adds additional estimated points between known sampled points of a digitally sampled pipe signal. This process gives greater definition to the analog sound wave sent to the speakers, reduces digital noise, and makes the reproduced sound seem more realistic.

LSI circuits (Large Scale Integrated circuits) - Computer chips that contain multiple transistors and performs logic functions. These chips are normally made of silicon and form the support for the transistors that are part of the circuit.

Leslie speaker - The speaker developed by Don Leslie for use with the Hammond organ. The rotating conical speakers at the top of the speaker cabinet creates the vibrato effect. This vibrato effect is increased in intensity by increasing the speed of the rotation.

Looping - If long samples are not used (longer than 10 seconds), the process of looping is used to lengthen the playback of the note on a digital organ beyond the length of the sample. If a note is held for 30 seconds, looping of a 10 second sample would be required.

Manual - The keyboard of an organ which is played by the hands. Manual keyboards usually contain 61 notes (5 octaves) instead of the 88 note keyboard of a piano. Most organs have two or three manuals, while very large organs may have four or five manuals. Only a few organs in the world have six or more manuals. Each manual can be selected to play a different division of the organ, such as Great, Swell, Choir, Solo, Antiphonal, etc.

MIDI (Musical Instrument Digital Interface) - A format used for standardization and compatibility of digital keyboards. This format was developed in the 1980's by major digital keyboard companies. It is also integrated into electronic and pipe organs.

Microprocessor - Computer chips that perform logic functions that were once performed by LSI's. These chips are the central processing units of computers and perform computation and logic functions. Microprocessors perform functions such as digital to analog conversion, digital sound processing and sample interpolation.

Mixture stops - Stops that have multiple ranks of pipes and are used to add brilliance to the principal chorus. They are designated by a Roman numeral. For example, "Mixture IV" is a mixture stop that has four ranks of pipes. Each key of the 61 note keyboard plays four notes for Mixture IV which represent pitches in the harmonic series rather than concert pitch. Therefore, a Mixture IV stop contains 244 pipes.

Non-volatile memory - A solid state memory storage device that does not require an external power source. This type of memory assists computers in the boot-up process in which commands are needed to direct the computer to execute functions of the operating system. This device functions using transistors and does not contain moving parts. The materials used in non-volatile memory chips are able to maintain required electronic charges to function for up to 10 years. A specific type of non-volatile memory is known as flash memory. The Intel Corporation is a leader in the development in non-volatile memory solutions, which is used primarily in wireless cell phones, but also has applications in digital organs. (For more information, see the Intel Corporation website: www.intel.com.)

Organ Console - The control center of the organ containing the keyboards, stop controls and coupling devices. The sound generating hardware and software for electronic organs is contained within the console. The organ speakers are only contained within consoles of very small organs. Most electronic organs have external speakers. In tracker organs, the console is part of the organ case because the entire instrument is mechanically linked. The use of electro-pneumatic controls allows the organ console to be detached from the pipe chambers.

Pedal organ - The division of the organ that plays bass notes. The pedal board is located under the console and is played by the feet.

Pipe - Column of metal or wood of a length corresponding to pitch. It is the sound source in pipe organs. Pipes are further classified as flue or reed pipes.

Pistons - Numbered or lettered buttons below the keyboards that allow combinations of organ voices (stops) to be saved. Pressing a piston brings on the corresponding preselected group of stops. Combination pistons can control the entire organ or individual divisions. Pistons also control couplers or other features of the organ, such as Tutti or Sforzando.

Positiv/Positive division - A division of the organ that is played from the bottom manual of the three-manual organ; it contains flue and reed stops and is not under expression. It is a smaller, less robust version of the Great division.

Praise and Worship Music (Contemporary) - Music used in contemporary Christian worship settings that uses less formal lyrics than traditional hymns. This type of music is usually accompanied by keyboards, guitars, drums and brass.

Principal - A foundational stop of the organ. It has a brighter sound than the diapason. The principal chorus is comprised of principal stops at the 16', 8', 4' and 2' pitches.

Rank - A complete set of pipes of an organ stop for each note on the keyboard. The low C note of an 8' principal stop is 8 feet long. The remaining 60 pipes in the 61 pipe principal rank are both shorter and narrower, and correspond to each note on the manual keyboard.

Reed pipe - the tone is created by a vibrating brass reed tongue. The pipe above the reed block acts as a resonator. The pitch of the reed pipe is related to the length of the resonator.

Reverberation system - Software used in electronic organs that simulates the acoustics of a pipe organ in a cathedral or other reverberant room.

Sample rate - The amount of digital information per second that is recorded from a real pipe sample. The higher the sample rate, the more nuances of the pipe sound that are captured in the sample. A sample with 20 bits/second will have more fidelity than one with 10 bits/second.

Sampling - The process of taking detailed recordings of organ pipes by converting the analog original pipe sound into a digital representation. The fidelity of the sampling is a function of the sampling rate (samples per second) and the sample precision (gradations of amplitude). A pipe sample may be as short as 10 seconds, starting with the initial sound of the pipe speaking to steady state and decay.

Semiconductor - A material that acts both as an electrical insulator and an electrical conductor. Transistors and diodes are made using these types of materials. Silicon is an example of a semiconductor.

Sforzando - Full organ sound brought on by a piston that activates preselected stops. This combination includes most of the stops on the organ with most of the couplers engaged. This combination can be set by the organist on many organs.

Solid State Electronics - Electronic devices made using semiconductor material that function as an amplifier, tone generator or rectifier. Examples of solid state electronic devices are transistors and diodes. Solid state electronic devices contain no moving electrical components.

Solo division - The division of the organ that is played from the top manual on a four-manual organ. This division contains solo stops such as Trumpet en chamade, Tuba, French horn, English horn and Corno di bassetto. If a 2 or 3-manual organ contains a solo division, it can usually be played from either manual using couplers.

Stop - An individual voice on the organ representing of a unique sound; the corresponding rank (or ranks) of pipes controlled by the drawknobs or stop tabs.

Stopjambs- The angled section of the organ console on each side of the manuals that contains the drawknob stop controls. The Great, Choir (or Positiv) and Solo division drawknobs are located in the stopjambs on the right. The Pedal and Swell division drawknobs are located in the stopjambs to the left of the manual keyboards. Drawknobs for other divisions are located in stopjambs on either side.

Swell division - The expressive division of the organ that contains principal, string, reed, flute and mutation stops. The ranks of pipes within the Swell division are contained within the Swell box. The

Swell division is played by the top manual on a two or three-manual organ.

Swell box - The enclosure for ranks of pipes within the Swell division. Openings in the Swell box are covered by Swell shutters or louvers which are controlled by the Swell pedal on the organ console. The volume of the Swell division is controlled by opening or closing the Swell shutters. These shutters or louvers look like the large vertical blinds used on patio doors and are each about 3" wide.

Tilt Tabs/rocker tabs - Stop controls that are pressed down to select the stop. The name of each stop and pitch level are indicated on the tab. The tabs for each division are arranged together above the organ keyboards. Similar to drawknobs, some tabs move while others light to indicate selection of the corresponding stop or coupler.

Toe pistons - Pistons located above the Pedal board that duplicate general pistons and pistons for the Pedal division. Reversible toe pistons usually select and remove 32' Pedal stops and Tutti or Sforzando for the entire organ.

Tone Generator - An electronic device that produces the organ tone in an electronic organ. These generators produce the tones for each rank of pipes of the organ. For older analog organs, vacuum tubes and then transistors were the tone generators. In digital organs, the tone generators are the stored memory of samples of actual organ pipes.

Tone Wheel - The means of sound generation in a vintage Hammond organ. The wheel is about the size of a silver dollar that has nicked edges and rotates at varying speeds. The tones produced are a function of the distance between the nicks in the edges and the speed at which the tone wheel rotates. This system of sound generation was invented by Laurens Hammond. Hammond organs built after the early 1970's use digital tone wheel sound generation rather than the tone wheels. This method proved more cost effective than original tone wheel generation.

Tracker organ - An organ that is controlled by a system of mechanical linkages or "trackers" that links keys played on the keyboard to the corresponding pipes for drawn stops. The key desk and pedals on a tracker organ are part of the organ case. Tracker organs were first built during the Baroque period in Germany.

Transistor - A solid state electrical device that functions as a tone generator, switch or amplifier. It is made using semiconductor materials of different polarities that result in flow of current through a circuit.

Tutti- Full organ sound brought on by pressing the Tutti piston which controls a preselected group of stops; synonymous with Sforzando.

Vacuum Tube - A tube in which electrical elements are contained in a gas. They were used as amplifiers, rectifiers (converts ac to dc) or tone generators in early electronic organs. As the tube warms, the signal current impacts the grid element which produces the amplified output current.

Velocity Sensitive Keyboards - Keyboards on digital organs since the late 1990's that have the capability of responding to the speed in which the keys are played for MIDI voices. The MIDI voices have the capability of responding to over 100 levels of speed input for the key played.

Vibrato - Variation in tone that creates a wavering or undulating effect; normally used with solo voices on an organ. Vibrato is also used to give the organ a more "gospel" or "theater" organ sound when used with full registrations.

Bibliography

Abbington, James, Let Mt. Zion Rejoice: Music in the African American Church, Judson Press, 2001.

"The Organs and the Carillon of the Crystal Cathedral," Crystal Cathedral Ministries, 2000.

Davis, Roger E., The Organists' Manual: Technical Studies and Selected Compositions for the Organ, W. W. Norton and Company, Inc., 1985.

Fine, Larry, The Piano Book, Brookside Press, 3rd Ed., 1995.

Kakehashi, Ikutaro, I Believe in Music: Life Experiences and Thoughts on the Future of Electronic Music by the Founder of the Roland Corporation, Hal Leonard Corporation, 2002.

Mapson, J. Wendell, Jr., The Ministry of Music in the Black Church, Judson Press, 1984.

Markowitz, Jerome, Triumphs and Trials of an Organ Builder, Allen Organ Company, 1989.

Ogasapian, John K., Church Organs: A Guide to Selection and Purchase, American Guild of Organists and Organ Historical Society Publishing, 1990.

Pellman, Samuel, An Introduction to the Creation of Electroacoustic Music, International Thomson Publishing, 1994.

Vail, Mark, The Hammond Organ: Beauty in the B, 2nd Ed., Backbeat Books, 2002.

Walker, Wyatt Tee, The Soul of Black Worship: Preaching, Praying, Singing, Martin Luther King Fellows Press, 1984.

Warren, Rick, The Purpose Driven Church: Growth Without Compromising Your Message & Mission, Zondervan, 1995.

Whitney, Craig R. All the Stops: The Glorious Pipe Organ and Its American Masters, Public Affairs, 2003.

End Notes

Introduction

1. Warren, Rick, Purpose Driven Church, Zondervan, 1995. p. 290.

2. Yoido Full Gospel Church Website.

Chapter 2

1. Whitney, Craig R., All The Stops, Public Affairs, 2003, p. XIV.

2. Davis, Roger E., The Organists Manual, W. W. Norton and Company, Inc, 1985. pp. 187-201. In addition to containing technical exercises and a wide selection of organ music, this work contains an excellent discourse on organ construction and stops. The diagrams of organ pipes in the book are very descriptive as well.

3. Whitney, p. 187-214.

4. Whitney, p. 161-185.

Chapter 3

1. Ochse, Orpha, The History of the Organ in the United States, Indiana University Press, 1975, p. 364-367.

2. Schantz Organ Company website.

3. Ochse, p. 327-328.

4. Ibid., p. 368-369.

5. Ibid., p. 328.

6. Ibid., p. 328.

7. Ibid., p. 379.

8. Ibid, p. 380-385.

9. Ochse, pp. 387-391.

10. Whitney, Craig R., All The Stops, Public Affairs, 2003, p. 226-234.

11. Ibid., p. 235-239.

12. Ochse, p. 368. Information on these organs was also obtained through several websites, to include Full Organ Company.

13. Robert. M. Turner Company Website.

14. Vail, Mark, The Hammond Organ: Beauty in the B, 2nd Ed., Backbeat Books, 2002., pp. 8-14, 128-136.

15. Ochse, p. 371-373.

16. Markowitz, Jerome, Trials and Triumphs of an Organ Builder, Allen Organ Company, 1984, p. 70-92.

17. Rodgers Instrument Corporation Website. The updated site contains a history of the Rodgers Organ Company as well as a Technical Glossary with many useful definitions.

18. Kakehashi, Ikutaro, I Believe in Music, Hal Leonard Corporation, 2002, p. 29-38.

19. Ibid.,p. 91-98.

20. Ibid., p. 176.

21. Ibid, p. 113, 171-184, 255-268.

Chapter 4

1. Rodgers Instrument Corporation Website.

2. Vail, Mark,The Hammond Organ: Beauty in the B, 2nd Ed., Backbeat Books, 2002, pp. 128-136.

3. Rodgers Instrument Corporation Website. The Website contains specifics on the Rodgers Audiophile Speakers. Technical specifications are found in the Rodgers speakers pamphlet.

4. Allen Organ Company Website. Contains links to the Legacy Audio website. Allen Herald speaker pamphlet contains technical specifications.

5. Walker Technical Company. Conversation with Bob Walker, founder of the company, in April 2003.

6. Kakehashi, Ikutaro, I Believe in Music, Hal Leonard Corporation, 2002, p. 174.

7. "The Organs and the Carillon of the Crystal Cathedral," Crystal Cathedral Ministries, 2000. This booklet contains the history and photos of the various organs on the campus of the Crystal Cathedral. An exhaustive stoplist of the Hazel Wright Organ is included as well.

8. Rodgers Instrument Corporation Website.

9. Organ Clearing House Website. This site contains listings of used pipe organs for sale and has been used to conduct a cost analysis.

10. This information was found at www.fullorgan.com, which is maintained by D.G. Dauphinee, an organ console designer who was perhaps the last employee of the M.P. Moller Organ Company.

Chapter 5

1. Steinway and Sons Piano Company Website.

2. Baldwin Piano Company Website

3. Kakehashi, Ikutaro, I Believe in Music, Hal Leonard Corporation, 2002, p. 186-201.

4. Warren, Rick, The Purpose Driven Church, Zondervan, 1995, p. 290.

5. Kakehashi, p. 196-198.

6. Rodgers 960 Users Manual and Rodgers PR-300S Users Manual.

Chapter 6

1. Associated Pipe Organ Builders of America (APOBA) Website.

2. Austin Organ Company Website.

3. Casavant Freres Website.

4. C. B. Fisk, Inc. Website.

5. OrganFocus.com Website.

6. Fratelli Ruffatti Website.

7. Schantz Organ Company Website.

8. Allen Organ Company Website.

9. Allen Organ Company Website.

10. Rodgers Instruments, LLC Website.

11. Rodgers Instruments, LLC Website.

12. Walker Technical Company. Conversation with Bob Walker, founder of the company in April 2003.

Chapter 7

1. This information was obtained through conversations with John Acker, President of Acker Organ Company.

2. Information on C.B. Fisk, Inc. Opus 124 was obtained from an informational brochure from C.B. Fisk, Inc.

3. Information on this great organ was obtained from a brochure published by Marshall Ogletree Associates.

Chapter 8

1. While at the Naval Academy from 1988-1992, I sang in the Protestant Chapel Choir, under the direction of Dr. John Talley. I also sang in the Gospel Choir, which was directed by Dr.

Joyce Garrett for my last two years. Much of the information here is based on personal experience. The Robert Pierce Company website also adds additional information.

2. This information is based on a conversation with Dr. Talley following the morning worship service at the USNA Chapel on May 15, 2005.

Printed in the United States
50073LVS00001B/52-153